CONTROVERSIAL TRANSITIONS

CONTROVERSIAL TRANSITIONS

MOFFAT DAVID

MiReads

Contents

I

Prologue

Loss of loved ones is painful and traumatic and all types of loss trigger questions to which there are rarely answers.

But in spite of this natural challenge there are yet other types of death which are in their very own category and require special attention. These relate to the deaths of the unborn, through miscarriage and abortion, and the hopeless who take their own lives.

They raise so many questions, resulting in confusion and controversy. Mostly, because we ought to have easy answers even from the word of God, but interestingly not many of us may be clear on this, even based on the Bible.

I answer those questions in this book using critical thinking and deduction from the truths and revelations that already exist in God's word. It is my hope that you will find peace as you battle with these questions and that the revelation which, I believe,

I have received from God's word, will illuminate your heart with peace and perhaps even joy and lead you into God's comforting embrace!

Moffat David
FCCA, CA(Mw) (CGEIT), B Acc.

2

Dedication

Sean and Aretha
'You are my joy'

Debbie.
'forever cherished .... take care of and name our little one'

'All those who have lost the unborn and those that have lost
loved ones to hopelessness
May God comfort you!'

3

Premature transition

Transition, or death, can sometimes occur prematurely. Medically, this means when death happens before the average age of death for any population or nation. This differs from country to country but in general it means 'something that is too soon or uncommonly early'.

Premature death is, however, not simply defined as unpalatable death because death is naturally unpalatable. Unpalatable death can be one that is unexpected, sudden, death of the young, of those that are newly born, or unborn or even of newlyweds for example. It can simply mean an undesired death. And this is characteristic of all death and normally it's regardless of the circumstance.

So, what is premature death? Well, spiritually, I think it means something else. I personally believe it is when we die before the days that God himself has set for us, but more importantly it is when we die without achieving the purpose we were meant to achieve on this earth. An example is the potential infant death of Jesus. When he was still a baby, Herod wanted to kill him by killing all toddlers of his age because Herod felt threatened by the prospect of another king who may potentially overthrow him, or so he thought (Mathew 2:16-18).

If Joseph and Mary would have exercised their rights to freedom and societal honor, they might have chosen to abort Jesus. It would have been an unplanned pregnancy and an intrusion into their courtship, according to today's logic Jesus was an unwanted child. And if aborted, where would we be today?

Pharaoh commanded that all male children under a certain age be killed! And if Jesus had been killed at this time, he would not have become the Savior of the world. If Jesus did not know the word of God when he was tempted by Satan to fall from the pinnacle of the temple, he would have died a foolhardy death and not a sacrificial death on the cross. So, I believe that we are all on a mission to fulfill the purpose of God in our lives and this mission has a timeframe in which it must be achieved. If we die before achieving this purpose, we have died prematurely!

Our purpose was foreordained according to scripture

"For we are his workmanship, created in Christ Jesus unto good works, which God hath before ordained that we should walk in them." Ephesians 2:10 KJV

And according to psalm 139 this purpose was allowed a timeframe.

"You saw me before I was born. Every day of my life was recorded in your book. Every moment was laid out before a single day had passed." Psalms 139:16 NLT

This means immediately we are born, there is a countdown timer that is running and counting down every second that passes by, every breath you breathe, and every heart beat you beat.

Because of this we ought to cry like the psalmist cried saying *"O my God, do not take me away in the midst of my days." Psalms 102:24 AMP.*

The rest of the book is arranged into three major segments that deal with death of infants, suicide, and pandemics.

Book 1 - Transition of infants and the unborn

4

What it is

Transition of infants and the unborn is probably one of the saddest types of transition. Unfortunately, it happens often. This is a type of premature transition but definitely requires its own discussion. I have also decided to discuss this to assist families that have experienced loss of infants and the unborn and also to understand why often times the transition of such is indeed premature.

THE SPIRIT COMES IN THE WOMB

The debate exists and still remains of 'when the spirit of a child comes into its body'. Some say when he is fertilized, some when he is a foetus and yet others believe at the point of birth. I think the Bible has a view of when this happens.

'As you do not know the way the spirit comes to the bones in the womb of a woman with child, so you do not know the work of God who makes everything.' Ecclesiastes 11:5

First, we see that the answer to this question is a mystery, but in spite of it being a mystery, one thing is clear, *the spirit comes in the womb of the woman,* and into the very bones of the child. This tells us that the baby is a human being while it is still in the womb.

For those who have miscarried before, I would like you to know that you have not completely lost your little baby. No matter at what stage the miscarriage occurred. You will see that child one day in heaven!

In fact, there is a well-known story of the Burpo family whose son almost died and went to heaven. According to the New York Times, in the true story published on April 27, 2012, and the related movie 'Heaven is for Real', Colton Burpo had a burst appendix and was rushed into surgery. After surgery Colton told his Dad, who had been praying fervently for him, that 'Daddy I almost died'.

When they came home, they discovered that Colton actually went to heaven and met Jesus. He also met a little girl who simply smiled at him and hugged him affectionately.

As he explained his experience, he asked his mom that 'do you know I have a sister?'

His mom answered yes to the question and thought he was talking of the sister he plays with, to which he answered *'no mom I have a big sister in heaven! She is 5 years old and she told me she died before she was born.'*

Astonished at this, Colton's mom remembered her miscarriage, and the age of the girl fit perfectly with the time of the miscarriage five years ago. But they had never told this to their son.

'What's her name', she asked

'She doesn't have a name mommy, she said you never named her because you did not know whether it was a boy or a girl'

Then his mom confirmed to him that indeed this happened and indeed they were unable to name the child as explained.

Medically, the sex of a baby can be known within 18 to 21 weeks but can even be as early as 14 weeks. This miscarriage therefore happened before 14 to 18 weeks and so we can deduce that even at that point God had already placed his spirit in this child. In fact, it is believed that once the woman's egg is fertilized and carried in the womb, the breath of life is already put within us. And medically it takes only about 21 days for a baby's heart to start beating and, if I may add, to start beating with God's breath of life.

The Burpo story is a real-life confirmation, that you need not despair because God put his spirit and breath of life in them and your baby is in heaven! If you have experienced loss through a miscarriage you can thank God that you will see them one day.

5

Identity and purpose of infants

Purpose is not something that we stumble upon. Purpose is something we were made to do in this life.

When we come on earth, we already have a purpose in the mind of God! The very thought of this means you are already known by God. This purpose stands ready for you to be born so it may start to slowly unfold!

This is explained in Ephesians 2:10 which emphasizes that even before the world came to be, God had already foreordained us for his divine purposes.

The Bible talks of a few people who were said to have purpose, even as either the unborn or infants.

Shall I speak of Jeremiah? who was told that he was consecrated to God while he was not yet born and still in his mother's womb?

"Before I formed you in the womb I knew you,
and before you were born I consecrated you;
I appointed you a prophet to the nations." Jeremiah 1:5

Shall I speak of Jacob and Esau who were known by God and whose destinies were known?

"And Isaac prayed to the LORD for his wife, because she was barren. And the LORD granted his prayer, and Rebekah his wife conceived. The children struggled together within her, and she said, "If it is thus, why is this happening to me?" So, she went to inquire of the LORD. And the LORD said to her,

"Two nations are in your womb,
and two peoples from within you shall be divided;
the one shall be stronger than the other,
the older shall serve the younger."

When her days to give birth were completed, behold, there were twins in her womb." Genesis 25:21-24

Shall I speak of John the Baptist? Whose birth was also foretold even before he was born. First, he was prophesied about in the book of Malachi as the prophet God would send to prepare a way for the Lord. Then he was announced by an angel to a barren couple of a priest and his wife who were both advanced in age. Several things were foretold about John's agenda

His gender would not be left to chance but would be known as a boy

His name would come from heaven - he would be called John

He would be a joy and a delight

He would be mighty and great in God's eyes

He would be filled with God's Holy Spirit

He would bring back many to the Lord their God

The Lord filled both Elizabeth and the child with the Holy Spirit while still in the womb.

"But the angel said to him, "Do not be afraid, Zacharias, for your prayer is heard; and your wife Elizabeth will bear you a son, and you shall call his name John. And you will have joy and gladness, and many will rejoice at his birth. For he will be great in the sight of the Lord, and shall drink neither wine nor strong drink. He will also be filled with the Holy Spirit, even from his mother's womb. And he will turn many of the children of Israel to the Lord their God. He will also go before Him in the spirit and power of Elijah, 'to turn the hearts of the fathers to the children,' and the disobedient to the wisdom of the just, to make ready a people prepared for the Lord."

And it happened, when Elizabeth heard the greeting of Mary, that the babe leaped in her womb; and Elizabeth was filled with the Holy Spirit." Luke 1:13-17, 41 NKJV

Importantly, at this time John is not yet conceived and yet all these things are being set out for him. His agenda and mission are being laid out. He also took time to elaborately describe the type of ministry John would have. The other thing that happened when John was actually conceived was his baptism with the Holy Spirit.

Shall I also talk of Samson? Whose birth was announced by an angel before his conception? Whose purpose as a Nazareth was clear at the time of announcement?

"Now there was a certain man from Zorah, of the family of the Danites, whose name was Manoah; and his wife was barren and had no children. And the Angel of the LORD appeared to the woman and said to her, "Indeed now, you are barren and have borne no children, but you shall conceive and bear a son. Now therefore, please be careful not to drink wine or similar drink, and not to eat anything unclean. For behold, you shall conceive and bear a son. And no razor shall come upon his head, for the child shall be a Nazirite to God from the womb; and he shall begin to deliver Israel out of the hand of the Philistines."" Judges 13:2-5 NKJV

Lastly, shall I talk of Jesus Christ? Whose birth was foretold numerous times in the Bible? We also learn a few things about Jesus

His name would come from heaven - 'he would be called Jesus'
He would be great
His gender as a man was certain
He would be a great light for the salvation of many
He would be king and sit on the throne of David according to Luke

1

And of Jesus there are numerous prophesies of who he is as 'a the suffering servant, the servant of the Lord, the root of Jesse, a child who would be born a king and the Government would be upon his shoulders, and also it is prophesied that Jesus was known well before his time on earth, in fact it is as early as 500 years when he is mentioned in Isaiah 9 and much earlier in the garden of Eden when he is referred to as 'the seed of the woman who shall strike the serpents head! Others have counted up to 33 to 55 direct prophecies of Jesus while some have noticed all other references to Jesus to be up to 351 instances in the Bible's Old Testament alone. This is phenomenal! That's how much God valued Jesus, and how he values even us even before we were born.

Listen to me, O coastlands,
and give attention, you peoples from afar.
The LORD called me from the womb,
from the body of my mother he named my name. Isaiah 49:1

What are we saying with all these arguments? God knows the little baby in your womb. And has already assigned an agenda for their life.

God gives your baby the spirit of life at the point of fertilization. When that first heartbeat happens in 21 days from conception, God has already put his breath in that child! Also, God has already named him.

Death of such a human being is a loss of the divine purposes of God that were meant for the blessing of this world. If you ever lose an infant or a child, I want you to know that you did not just loose a foetus, you lost a child, a future lawyer, or engineer or preacher. You have not lost someone who is unimportant. They are important to God! The consolation however is that they are in God's presence! And most of all they are not lost!

6

God's involvement in the womb

God is so involved in our development even when we are unborn. The Bible talks of this and the fact that God has numerous plans for us

For you formed my inward parts;
you knitted me together in my mother's womb.
I praise you, for I am fearfully and wonderfully made.
Wonderful are your works;
my soul knows it very well.
My frame was not hidden from you,
when I was being made in secret,
intricately woven in the depths of the earth.
Your eyes saw my unformed substance;

in your book were written, every one of them,
the days that were formed for me,
when as yet there was none of them.
How precious to me are your thoughts, O God!
How vast is the sum of them!
Psalms 139:13-17

Though the unborn seem hidden away in the mother's womb, God is so interested in their wellbeing. He knits them together, he intricately weaves our flesh, skin and bones!

The unborn is naturally hidden from the world but is not hidden from God! So, the passage says, '*my frame was not hidden from you when I was being made in secret*'.

Something interesting here is that God sees us when our substance is yet unformed. That would indicate that he sees us even when we are just a fertilized embryo and later as a foetus, and while the body parts are still unformed, we are already acknowledged and noticed and seen by God. In other words, our spirit is already in that egg. In fact, Job had this insight already when he tells God that

"Have You not poured me out like milk And curdled me like cheese? [You have] clothed me with skin and flesh, And knit me together with bones and sinews." Job 10:10-11 AMP

Interestingly, Job talks of the process that starts with being poured out like milk. Just as the milk of life is poured into the womb of a woman as sperm, Job makes an interesting parallel here. Just as milk is curdled to make cheese he describes how we too are curdled in the womb. Now... to curdle means to clot, coagulate, to thicken and solidify. This speaks of the embryonic stage of our development in which cell division and multiplication occurs. This speaks of the milk that now solidifies into curdles or cells that later develop into organs and then into limbs. Job summarizes this process by saying he was given clothing of skin and flesh and that he was knit together with structures to give him both support and mobility, which are bones and muscle.

Interestingly, and most importantly, he reveals to us two things, firstly that ***'he is not his body'*** in other words the body is not the real person, as a matter of fact he plainly says his body is simply ***'a piece of clothing!'*** Secondly, he is, therefore, saying that he is actually a Spirit who was placed into the body at the time of fertilization and he describes the process as through the eyes of a spirit who is observing and marveling at the creative power of his God! In other words, he was breathed into the womb of his mother and actually existed before his body was fully manufactured! Job reveals to us that he did not exist when his heart started beating or when the body parts formed fully, but way way before! And, he even marveled at the creation process of God in the womb from beginning to end, from the point of fertilization in the womb when he was poured out like milk as sperm, to the time he cried his first cry at the point of birth. The conclusion of the matter is that your baby exists as a full spirit with purpose from the point he is planted in the womb! No two ways about it!

HOW GOD KNITS US IN THE WOMB

The process that Job explains is backed by science and is described further below.

The normal baby development is that by 4 weeks (1 month) , your baby is an embryo consisting of two layers of cells from which all body parts and organs develop through cell multiplication, by 8 weeks (2 months) it is the size of a kidney bean, is constantly moving and has a head and distinct but webbed hands, feet and fingers, at 12 weeks (3 months) they are more distinct, and is the size of a pea pod with unique god given fingerprint identifiers.

All this time the child has rubbery cartilage which God transforms to bone by 16 weeks (4 months). At 20 weeks (5 months) God ensures that eyebrows and eyelids are in place and the baby is about 27cm or 10.5in. At 24 weeks (6 months) your baby is weighing about 660g while at 28 weeks (7 months) the baby is 40cm and can open and close her eyes and possibly see around him.

By 32 weeks (8 months) God prepares the baby for the outside world by developing his lungs fully and has a weight of about 2.2 kg (4.7 lb.).

In 36 weeks, God has finished his masterpiece of a child and the baby is almost due for birth and will be 51 cm weighing up to about 3.4 kg (7.5lb). And, with much anticipation and excitement he gives you a gift of a lovely child.

"children are a gift from the Lord; They are a reward from him."
Psalms 127:3 ASV

"Lo, children are a heritage of Jehovah; And the fruit of the womb is his reward." Psalms 127:3 ASV

7

How the unborn transition prematurely

The unborn and newly born infants can succumb to various medical and social dangers that can, sadly, take their lives.

Medically, a certain proportion of pregnancies result in miscarriage. This can be from a range of medical causes.

There are also some babies who succumb to still birth and others who succumb to various challenges in the first year and first few years of birth.

The best recommendation I can make during pregnancy is to get the necessary prenatal care. The same applies for post-natal care which you can receive after the birth of the child and also to rely on God's enabling grace as you do your very best. And, I believe, God will bless the work of your hands and the fruit of your womb.

The unborn can also experience loss of life due to medical or elective terminations. Medical terminations usually occur when the life of the mother is at risk due to the pregnancy. Elective terminations occur when the parents of the child have decided to terminate the pregnancy.

The reasons for such terminations include unplanned pregnancies especially those occurring at times when the pregnancy is expected to interfere with personal plans of education, relationships and social pressures in general due to taboos surrounding underage pregnancy or pregnancy out of wedlock and even pregnancy as a result of infidelity for those held in very high, political, social and spiritual esteem . There is also a big social taboo of incest and rape. The bottom line with such terminations is that the pregnancy is largely inconvenient for all these various reasons.

SHOULD WE PROTECT THE UNBORN?

There is strong debate regarding whether or not elective terminations are right or wrong. And whether we should at all protect the rights of the unborn versus the elective rights of the mother or the parent.

When you look at the Bible and the discussion we have had so far, some things cannot be ignored. What can't be ignored is the fact that God is always involved in our lives from conception and even long before. God also puts his spirit in our bones when we are yet unformed, and he sees us in this state.

The 'seeing' we're talking about is not just physical seeing, but progresses from recognition, to noticing and taking interest and acknowledging our identity and purpose.

He puts life in us from conception and then tells us that 'thou shall not kill'.

We also see that God has a purpose for each child and to terminate this life is to go against the purposes of God and to frustrate the plans of God.

People argue that we should protect the woman's right and that it is her body. Well the woman's body is not her own, and according to scripture our bodies are temples of the Holy Spirit. You cannot do whatever you will with your body, actually, God promises that if you destroy it or defile it, God will also destroy you. In fact, your body is God's temple and God's property, and that little child within you is also God's temple and God's property. And electing to terminate its life is electing to terminate an innocent temple that doesn't belong to you. This is a sin of double jeopardy! Defilement of your body with death as a parent and destruction of an innocent temple, a sin which also requires its own judgement!

Or do you not know that your body is a temple of the Holy Spirit within you, whom you have from God? You are not your own, for you were bought with a price. So, glorify God in your body. 1 Corinthians 6:19-20

Do you not know that you are God's temple and that God's Spirit dwells in you? If anyone destroys God's temple, God will destroy him. For God's temple is holy, and you are that temple. 1 Corinthians 3:16-17

The little child within the womb also has a right to life. But what is life after all?

'Life is the condition that distinguishes animals and plants from inorganic matter, including the capacity for growth, reproduction, functional activity, and continual change preceding death'.

When you use this dictionary definition of life can you conclude that the foetus is not alive when it has functional activity of growth and development, and when it is continually changing? I think not!

It's very much alive! In fact, if it were not alive there would be a natural miscarriage. The human body does not carry dead things without rejecting and expelling them. Therefore, this little child at whatever stage has a right to life according to Article 3 of the United Nations Universal Declaration of Human Rights. Why does it have the right to life? The right to life is for those who are already alive! If the unborn child is alive, then it has a right to life! This is a right for the living alone.

As we have seen, some believe elective terminations should happen by legal right because of inconvenience, perhaps for various social and spiritual reasons including a sense of shame due to, sin, incest and rape. However, in response to this we know that God has instituted that 'everyone should die for his own sin' and therefore the sin mistakes or inconveniences of the fathers should not be punished on the child.

"Yet you say, Why should not the son suffer for the iniquity of the father?'

When the son has done what is just and right, and has been careful to observe all my statutes, he shall surely live. The soul who sins shall die. The son shall not suffer for the iniquity of the father, nor the father suffer for the iniquity of the son. The righteousness of the righteous shall be upon himself, and the wickedness of the wicked shall be upon himself. Ezekiel 18:19-20

"Fathers shall not be put to death because of their children, nor shall children be put to death because of their fathers. Each one shall be put to death for his own sin. Deuteronomy 24:16

This argument is not new, this scripture starts with a question why children should not suffer from the sins and inconveniences of the parent, and the reason is that each shall die for his own sins.

The unborn also need protection because naturally they are vulnerable. This protection comes from God and also god-fearing people.

'On you was I cast from my birth,
and from my mother's womb you have been my God.' Psalms 22:10

The unborn require our protection and God is particularly passionate about protecting children and the weak. The picture we have in this scripture is that of total dependence on God and the nursing mother. In such a vulnerable state the children and the unborn require our protection and God expects and demands this protection from us.

Therefore, we are to defend the weak and not take advantage of them. For this reason, God says

'Open your mouth for the mute,
for the rights of all who are destitute.
Open your mouth, judge righteously,
defend the rights of the poor and needy.' Proverbs 31:8-9

'do not kill the innocent and righteous, for I will not acquit the wicked.' Exodus 23:7

Did you know that the unborn and the little infants have angels and that these angels plead their case before God? This is another dangerous reason for you and me if we do not defend either the unborn or the weak

"See that you do not despise one of these little ones. For I tell you that in heaven their angels always see the face of my Father who is in heaven." Matthew 18:10

Elective terminations are by nature, unnatural and therefore they logically "go against the order of nature" and naturally... go against God. Most unnatural things require significant effort, risk and pain to both accomplish and propagate. As a result, for any termination to take place almost all the methods used are quite gruesome in reality and, I imagine, are quite traumatic on the child too.

Generally, abortions are broadly categorized into three categories of Surgical, medical and chemical abortions. All of which are traumatic, gruesome and ghastly on the child and should not be done by someone who is a protector of this innocent soul, whether mother or father.

Surgical termination methods generally involve either suction of the baby's vital amniotic fluid that provided protection and nutrients inducing trauma in the child. They then dismember the child by either barbaric tearing and pulling off the child's limbs from his body, and any part that the abortive instrument helps itself to, including the torso and finally the head which is also crushed until the brains ooze out as proof of a complete and 'successful' "*procedure*".

Other methods require straight forward cutting of the child's body, leading to shock and immense pain for the child. Whether dismembered by pulling or cut up by slicing, the body parts are laid on a tray and fully accounted for to ensure no part is left behind.

Medical and other indigenous terminations involve medicines that kill the child or breakdown the uterine lining so that the child is no longer supported or held in the womb, also it involves poisoning the child so that the child struggles and convulses for about an hour or two until it dies. Then they induce a premature birth to expel the child.

Chemical methods literally burn the child and or disintegrate it until it dies. This is what happens when salt and similar injections are used. A woman who performed an abortion was traumatized as she felt her little baby suffer from a salt injection abortion. She describes how her baby struggled as the salt burnt her baby's skin and throat like acid. The very fluid with which she used to breath and absorb nutrients now became an acidic and liquid fire that was swallowed down her throat. Covered in a fire of liquid salt her skin and organs were burnt alive at the stake and alter of abortion. She describes how her baby struggled for more than an hour, kicking and fighting for life. With a heavy heart she realized her error, in the midst of her guilt and shame, her motherly instinct kicked in. She wanted to care for and hold her baby, but she could only touch her tummy and speak comforting words to her child.

'You are not alone my child, I am with you my child, I'm sorry my child, mommy didn't know what she was doing, I am so sorry my child'

As she spoke these words the kicks in her womb grew dim, maybe in acceptance of her mother's apology, or maybe in pure defeat from her traumatic ordeal, but at the end of it all, the child succumbed to her fiery battle, as if fighting with molten lava all around her, and died. Shortly after, the abortionist who had left her all alone, went in to dismember her child and remove her from the womb. Leaving not just an empty womb but an empty heart in her mother's soul and a deep and dark shadow of guilt that would haunt her for the rest of her life.

What we see is that it takes significant effort to achieve something that is unnatural and that is, as we can see, very cruel on the child.

The mother who terminates a child's life also suffers a great deal because, normally, they will do it against their sense of right or wrong. Some will say that a feeling of guilt or sense of wrongdoing is only dependent on the moral teachings we hear through life, either from culture or faith, however, moral teaching aside we should know that the mother is naturally and hormonally geared to carry a child to term. Termination therefore will result in trauma because the natural mothering instinct and biological processes are forcefully and brutishly overridden.

There are many who downplay the effects of abortion but for you, don't be naive enough to ignore the reality of abortion regret. Some women bottle up their emotional pain for years and years. Some have their emotional struggle resurface after even 7 years or more. They regret that the initial need to be independent only brought them misery, shame, guilt and pain. The common effects that are seen arise from attempts to 'heal and numb the pain' and this manifests in a range of outcomes ranging from substance abuse, self-destructive behaviors and depression.

Some have been traumatized by visions in which the aborted children follow them around and asked why they were killed and not given a chance to live. I remember this was the case of one secondary school girl who asked for prayer, complaining that she never sleeps because every time she goes to bed and closes her eyes, she has this recurring vision which went on for more than two years until it stopped by prayer and forgiveness from God. Some relive the experience over and over again with nightmares of dismembered babies. The anniversary of your abortion also proves traumatic among other medical complications that arise from abortions. This stress has been medically diagnosed and described as post abortion stress syndrome (PASS).

A certain nurse who was working in an abortion clinic received a word from God through a dream that God will demand the blood of the innocents from her and that the price will be borne by her children. She immediately resigned from her abortion clinic and started working at a general hospital. She told her story to my sister in law who is also a nurse at the general hospital.

So, we see that killing and not defending the innocent is a great sin before God and is included among the great sins of the Bible

"There are six things that the LORD hates,
seven that are an abomination to him:
haughty eyes, a lying tongue,
and hands that shed innocent blood." Proverbs 6:16-17

So, what's the conclusion of this? You can make decisions on what you think is 'your body', but, in reality, is 'God's temple' and 'God's property', you can advance 'your rights' and ignore the rights of the unborn or you can protect them. You can be relied on by God to protect that innocent child or be an instrument that works against his gift of life and the purpose he has planted in the life of the unborn.

You can go to great lengths to hide your shame and your sin like David did with Bathsheba by committing murder to cover sin of an adulterous relationship and infidelity. I would rather you do not pile up error upon error or sin upon sin and simply be humble enough and man up to deal with the inconveniences and social challenges you are facing, because God can give you the wisdom and strength to deal with your situation by allowing the blood of Jesus to declare you righteous and forgiven by God. Or you can choose to attend to your conveniences and tear that little baby limb from limb or cut and slice up your little one. Or you can simply decide to attend to God's purposes. God is never frustrated even if you have been raped and made pregnant unwillingly, God has a purpose for that innocent soul, it was set beforehand but it's only the timing that was, potentially, wrong.

The choice, frankly, is yours. You can decide to live with the trauma and guilt of abortion, to defend your own rights but one thing is certain, you will not escape the consequences of abortion. Consequences of trauma, guilt and pain, and ultimately of answering before God. Remember we will all stand and give an account of our lives before God.

"So then, each of us will give an account of himself to God." Romans 14:12

"And no creature is hidden from his sight, but all are naked and exposed to the eyes of him to whom we must give account." Hebrews 4:13

"Rejoice, O young man, in your youth, and let your heart cheer you in the days of your youth. Walk in the ways of your heart and the sight of your eyes. But know that for all these things God will bring you into judgment." Ecclesiastes 11:9

So, whatever you decide please know that God is the ultimate democrat, he lets you do as you wish but he is also completely just and must reward you for your actions. Therefore, you will give an account of yourself one day. You cannot carry and embrace fire in your bosom and not be burnt!

But, I would rather you hear the command of God that says

'Rescue those who are being taken away to death;
hold back those who are stumbling to the slaughter.' Proverbs 24:1

8

Coping with loss of infants and the unborn

Lastly, I would like to talk about how couples can cope with a miscarriage.

I think it's important to know that miscarriages are largely outside of the control of the couple experiencing loss. They happen because of abnormalities in the fetus or the placenta and sometimes can be due to chromosome problems or due to the egg being attached in the wrong place leading to inability to be carried to term and an early miscarriage.

These are just the technical aspects of miscarriage, but it is usually accompanied by strong physical, emotional and spiritual effects on couples.

Physically, the woman's body will need to heal from the procedures performed as she was getting medical attention since the womb will be injured in the process.

Emotionally, there will be a great sense of loss regardless of the age of the pregnancy. Women will be most affected especially if the pregnancy was larger. However, all face a sense of loss. The challenge that exists is how the man should comfort his partner. Mostly, he will be unsure and fear that the woman believes he does not understand her fully. After all, she was the one carrying the child, and the one who had mood swings, cravings and related pregnancy effects on her body. It's important for women to be accommodating because men are simply trying to help, and they too were part of the pregnancy as they supported their partners with all their emotional and physical needs during the pregnancy. Even making unusual efforts to satisfy her sometimes weird cravings. A sense of loss will arise from shattered dreams of having a baby and, depending on the level of preparation, sometimes the baby room and supplies will be a constant reminder of this loss. This may lead to a sense of failure and despair.

Men are usually wired to fix things and the common temptation is to try to fix this. But something like this can't be fixed. In desperation we may be tempted to say, 'don't despair, we'll have other kids.' This is also a mistake that must be avoided because that child is unique and individually irreplaceable. The best is to simply stand by each other and let God handle your helplessness.

It is common to be fearful about falling pregnant on the basis that this may recur. While this fear is normal, it's important to trust in God as the author of life and know that your tragedy was something you could not control. Some women misunderstand the medical reasons for, and wrongly fear that it arose due to sex during pregnancy but there is no medical proof to support such fears of adverse effects of marital intimacy during pregnancy. There will be few cases where a delicate pregnancy may require the doctor to advise you to halt this for a few weeks but generally you will be advised to resume once the woman and the baby are out of danger and in some cases, it will only be precautionary.

The most important thing when dealing with this loss is not to blame each other or attribute the loss to medically unsound theories which may simply drive a wedge between your marital and emotional intimacy.

Spiritually, we all struggle to understand why bad things are happening to us, but much as you may not have an answer for everything, you need to settle it in your heart that God is a good God. And he is good all the time!

Do not let the enemy fool, you into thinking that God is punishing you for past sins or past abortions. When you are in Christ Jesus God promised to forgive you and not to condemn you even if you may have elected to terminate past pregnancies.

'There is therefore now no condemnation for those who are in Christ Jesus.' Romans 8:1

In fact, all the evil that happens in the world is because God's perfect world was affected by the sin and disobedience that Satan himself introduced in the world! He should take responsibility for all imperfections in this world as the one who comes but to steal, kill and destroy! Don't let the enemy fool you into this lie, he is after all, the father of lies!

I believe that God will increase your understanding of things and will help you to grow in wisdom as you navigate the stormy seas of your loss.

Book 2 -Transition of the hopeless

9

What it is

Transition of the hopeless is a sad type of transition. It is not an abortion of the unborn but an abortion of 'the born', of those that are fully alive and, sadly, it's an abortion of purpose.

This introduction is actually a conclusion and, if truth be told, I need not say more. I am compelled, however, to proceed because such a transition is one of the most traumatic not only for those who transition but more so for those who are left behind.

Transition of the hopeless is a transition of those who have died prematurely because they have lost hope in life. This happens to those who are both healthy and are fighting disease.

I will call it ***'the battle of the soul'*** that eventually wears us down because of incessant pressures and concerns. The soul is a key battleground where fiery darts of various disorders, such as depression, anxiety and substance abuse, affect millions of people. The impact of this assault on the soul is premature mortality, degraded functioning and degraded quality of life.

THE GRAVITY OF THE PROBLEM

Premature mortality is often by means of suicide. This is generally described and accepted as 'the taking of one's own life'.

Though data varies depending on the source used, both, 'Our world in Data' and the 'World health organization' seem to agree that every 40 seconds someone around the world takes his own life and this is double the global murder rate. The problem is generally two times higher in men than in women but in other countries it's much more than this ratio of two times higher. In the developing world, in 2017, it was about 1.5 times higher while it was more than 3.5 times higher in the developed world.

This is a leading cause of death especially in young people and a number of reviews have found that there is an increased risk of suicide among transgender, lesbian, gay and bisexual people which lead to suicide attempts of about 40% compared to about 5% for the general population.

Recently we have seen increasing cases in our societies and even among people of whom we would least expect. These include very calm and respectable people, people of faith and, generally, people of repute in society. This is a problem most governments will not actively invest in because it is not seen as a priority. However, the more this happens, the more we will continue losing people to this problem that normally comes as a result of hopelessness.

Finally, for every completed suicide that occurs there are about 20 more attempts that occur but are not completed and every death leaves a significant ripple effect. The family is affected because they will suffer from the confusion of why this happened. This is especially so because the majority will not leave a note explaining why they took their lives because suicide notes are left by only about 40% of people who kill themselves.

The social stigma and shame for those left behind can also be unbearable. If any other death is confusing and traumatic enough for the affected family, I really can't imagine how much more confusing a suicide must be on any family. It must truly be deeply traumatic on children, parents, wives, husbands, brothers and sisters, friends and relatives in general.

THE ONSET OF HOPELESSNESS

Hope by its very nature is a word that is *'pregnant with expectation', because h*ope expects good things to happen.

Hope speaks of confidence, expectation, optimism, anticipation courage, boldness and audacity, faith and belief. It also speaks of opportunity, prospect, likelihood and possibility. It talks of promise and potential. In the realm of emotion, it talks of desire, of aspiration, dreams, passion, obsession, plans, wishes and goals.

Hope is a powerful word! I personally believe that hope is the womb in which faith is both nurtured and born. Hope is an atmosphere that makes it ready for expectation to ignite and crystallize in an instant. It makes faith to be born when the seed of God's word is planted in our hearts and without hope even faith cannot be born. Hope is a long term and durational phenomenon while faith can be short term and momentous. At specific moments in life God will speak a word that will fertilize the womb that is already conducive and fertile with hope so that that word produces fruit. Words will come from time to time, but the fertile atmosphere and womb of hope is always a constant for the seeds of faith and promise to grow. Hope is indispensable and hope is the essence of life itself! Hope is purpose and without it we are clueless of why we are here and where we are going. But when the purpose and promises of God's word impregnate our souls, we carry the unborn seed, the unborn spiritual child that we call faith and in due season this seed will flourish in this womb and finally be born in our beautiful world in fulfillment of God's purpose.

Hope is the weapon God has given you to 'soldier on' in life when the going gets tough. It is the reserve tank of energy that will take you the next 100 miles into and across the barren lands and wildernesses of adversity and sickness. Hope will literally rejuvenate not just your soul but your physical body!

Hope is a powerful weapon dreaded by Satan your enemy, and he is no ordinary enemy but your sworn enemy. He is a cruel task master who even kills his own soldiers through his demonic martial law. The fact that you are just a simple Christian and you do not serve God in serious ministry does not mean you will not anger and rouse him and your being a normal Christian certainly does not guarantee your safety. He will seek to destroy you and assault you every chance he gets. Even if it is to stop you dead in your tracks as you try to draw close to God in various Christian disciplines, habits and virtues as a mere child of God!

Satan is your sworn enemy and have no doubts about it! He has sworn to resist and oppose the kingdom of heaven and try to kill you every chance he gets. Not only to kill you but to abort your mission! If he cannot abort you in your mother's womb, he will definitely launch an assault on your soul. He'll try to wear you down, and to make you give up. He will launch the rocket propelled grenades and rockets of despair and hopelessness. Be under no illusion.... Satan is your sworn enemy and he wants to destroy you!

10

God's perspective on our assaults

THE IMPACT OF ASSAULT

When you really think of it, all the different torments and assaults on this battlefield called life can throw you completely off balance. They can affect your psyche and mental wellbeing. This stress can manifest in many different ways and lead to illnesses which by themselves can cause early death. There are those who will lose the will to live when assaulted by trials and temptations just like Job. And, like Job's wife they will conclude, and seemingly logically so, that it's better to curse God and die. They will find no reason for living and conclude that God is in fact a cruel and unloving God! Like Judas, their sin will seem so insurmountable that taking their lives seems only logical and deserving.

Like king Saul, the torment of their minds and agitating voices of rejection that whisper endlessly, night and day, wear them down to the extent that they no longer see the kindness of God and decide not to fight till the end but to 'end it now'.

Like Leah they carry a searing and burning coal of rejection too hot to handle and too heavy to bear!

I could go on and on! But I have news for you! Good news in fact... and this is that 'God is not done with you!'

GOD'S PLANS IN SPITE OF OUR ASSAULT

In the case of Leah, she was not only rejected but was also written-off as being unable to bear children for Jacob. So, when Rachel wanted to live her 'preferred life' of 'having everything and anything she wants', and when she could not take no for an answer to anything, God had a trick up his sleeve. And, as the Bible puts it, one day she saw something that wasn't hers but wanted it. Reuben, Leah's son, had some mandrakes (a plant with yellow berries. A fruit called Mayapple) and she craved them with her usual burning intensity.

Knowing that Leah was now past bearing age and was no threat to her she thoughtlessly offered Leah a night with 'her' husband and behold that night Leah 'the barren wife' conceived Issachar, a powerful tribe that all Israel would look up to because as the Bible puts it, 'they knew the times and told Israel what they ought to do' (1 Chronicles 12:32).

Actually, God was not done with her, and she had yet another child called Zebulun. In fact, Leah, the rejected Leah, was the more favored one in God's eyes. So, you might be rejected by men but know one thing, that you are favored and loved by God! Leah was in fact the woman who started bearing Jacob four children before Jacob's 'beloved Rachel' ever had children. And the reason was simple and divinely deliberate,

'When the LORD saw that Leah was hated, he opened her womb, but Rachel was barren.' Genesis 29:31

Whenever you are rejected by men you should know that God loves you! In fact, when you think about it, you could argue and agree with me that more of the most significant tribes in Israel came from Leah. Oh yes, think of Levi, the third born! They were priests that took care of the atonement and spiritual welfare of Israel for all times until this day! Talk of Judah the fourth born child, the tribe that brought forth Jesus the messiah, who is rightly called the Lion of the tribe of Judah! Think of Issachar a tribe that had the Spirit of Prophecy.

This does not mean Rebecca was completely sidelined by God because she too had a significant son named Joseph. And we all, know the story of Joseph who was rejected by his brothers and yet became king of Egypt and, with divine help, saved the whole world when God told him how to prepare for famine. Indeed, he literally saved the whole world. However even though she was the loved wife she really only bore Jacob 2 children and in fact she was taken away by God as she died in childbirth when giving birth to Benjamin and Leah lived on to have more of Jacob than Rachel ever had.

I want to tell you that you might be rejected and unloved, but God has a purpose for you. You still have a Levi, in you, you have an Issachar in you and most of all you have a Judah in you. There is a Jesus in you! Don't fret don't give up hope, don't despair like

Rachel saying 'give me, give me or I die' because now is not the time to die! Rachel may have written off Leah, but God had not written her off and he has not written you off! God will surprise your rivals! He is not done with you; don't you lose your will to live! Even if you don't bear a child of your own there is a Queen Esther you ought to raise. God has called you to raise that foster child, to adopt that orphan! You are ordained to raise kings and queens!

You might be a king Saul burdened with guilt and rejection, tormented with schizophrenia but, stand your ground and fight till the end! In fact, you might live to fight another day! The fact that you are being judged by God does not mean that God does not love you.

'For the Lord disciplines the one he loves,

and chastises every son whom he receives."

"Besides this, we have had earthly fathers who disciplined us, and we respected them. Shall we not much more be subject to the Father of spirits and live? For they disciplined us for a short time as it seemed best to them, but he disciplines us for our good, that we may share his holiness." Hebrews 12:6,9,10

God would rather beat the foolishness out of us than let us perish in our foolishness and loose our souls. We may be reeling with the effects of our errors but that does not mean he is an unloving God; he says he can make our sin as white as snow.

'Consequence' and 'forgiveness' are two different things. We may be forgiven but we may still face the consequences of our sin or error. That's why when we are judged by God, we should not mistake it for 'rejection' and 'condemnation'. And so, an unplanned pregnancy may still delay our education or make it a little more difficult, a work error may still cost us our job and infidelity will still result in lack of trust which must be rebuilt from scratch.

All in all, let's remember that when God judges us, he is disciplining us so we may enter his glory, so we may be better and 'share in his holiness'.

So.....fight even if it's your last stand, who knows what God can do in your last stand? Look at Samson, in his last stand he killed more of his enemies than when he was alive. Fight and pray like Samson prayed *'give me strength one last time oh God'.*

Like Judas, you may have sinned a grave sin, you may have gambled and lost it all, but don't despair God says, *"though your sins are as red as scarlet they will become whiter than snow!"*

If Jesus recommissioned Peter by whom he was rejected 3 times, don't you think he would have reached out to Judas too if he were alive? Would he not have left the 99 to seek the one?

I am always intrigued by the prodigal son. When we think about it, he effectively squandered his father's wealth and impoverished himself. Destroying your parents' empire is a big deal! But despite his mistakes the son remembered his father, the love and graciousness of his father and said, 'I will go back to my father'.

That's the attitude we ought to have. You have a father you can run to as well! A father who stands staring daily into the horizon for sons and daughters who would return to him. Those who have conquered their guilt and condemnation, those who raise their shield of faith when the enemy thrusts the sword of condemnation, hopelessness, panic and despair.

Like Job we should fight on and say I don't understand everything, but God is sovereign, he gives and takes away...

We should no longer curse the day we were born because God has a purpose for us!

You might be battling rejection but know that God has not rejected you! You feel you're at the end of the road but know that God is not done with you yet! And just like Leah, God will surprise you with what he has in store!

Like David we should declare that God protects us and has chosen us even though things are not going our way and we are opposed heavily. We should declare that *'you have laid your hand on me'*.

You should remind yourself always of the promise of God upon your life. You should also know that you are chosen and have purpose. Don't give up, don't say

'I am done for'

'I am in need' or

'I don't have so let me die!'

No! don't say

'I am tormented with lack of love, with rejection and judgement and God has no place for me in his kingdom'.

No! this is not the end! When those voices of condemnation whisper in your head, answer them with the loving promise of God, and the words of Jesus

'Come to me, all who labor and are heavy laden, and I will give you rest.' Matthew 11:28

You must declare like David

"Yet I am confident I will see the Lord's goodness while I am here in the land of the living." Psalms 27:13 NL

No matter what rages around you, or how high the waves billow over you, God wants you to be confident of just one thing! That you will see his goodness in this life!

But, to declare this, you must first believe that he is good! Remember he does not forsake his own! He is a kind God! He is a loving God. So, in this life... in the land of the living... you will see his goodness and you must say 'I too am confident, certain, believing and sure that I will see God's Goodness in this land of the living!

A CALL TO US WHO ARE WHOLE

Perhaps it's high time you and I stop shooting our very own wounded soldiers. Perhaps it's time to see the trauma of Lot's wife, the torment and depression of Saul, the despair and remorse of Judas who was poisoned with lies that all is doom and gloom. I think it's high time we pray for those who struggle with the will to live, those who are contemplating giving up to the devil. Perhaps it's high time we reach out to families traumatized by the scars of suicidal deaths. It's time we tell of '*how loving Jesus is*' to those who are weary and laden with fear and rejection, those confused by schizophrenia.

I cannot definitely tell you what happens when we take our own lives, we explore this in more detail in a different chapter. But I don't want to take that gamble, and neither should you.

All I can do is show you the master who has compassion on such people, who calls these people and tells them to find rest in Jesus. Who promises to lighten their burden!

So perhaps you and I should open our hearts to them and say, 'this condemnation of the church, this shooting of our wounded soldiers will no longer happen under my watch!'

11

The illusion of rest

The saddest thing about suicide is the illusion of rest and escape. An illusion is, sadly, something that we believe is there but is actually not or is false. Just like a mirage in a scorching desert, the traveler thinks he sees a lifesaving oasis where he will quench his thirst but as he approaches the mirage disappears and he remains famished under the scorching sun. Hopes are dashed at discovery of such falsehood and despair sets in when the reality dawns in them that they might have changed course to waste their final energies on this mirage. Possibly lost and dehydrated the chances of survival dwindle to next to none as they face almost certain death!

And those who commit suicide believe they are escaping pressure and going to a place of rest.... But do they really rest?

OUR LIFE OR GOD'S LIFE?

I think the fundamental question of whether suicide is right or wrong is based on 'whose life it is' that we are taking. When we know this, we know who ultimately 'has the power' to take or give life.

"then the dust [out of which God made man's body] will return to the earth as it was, and the spirit will return to God who gave it." Ecclesiastes 12:7 AMP

All through the Bible we find clues that tell us that 'we are not our own.' The breath we have was given to us as a gift and we ought to use this gift properly, wisely and to the honor of God who gave it.

It is not our own neither are we our own! We belong to God!

THOSE WHO DO NOT HAVE CHRIST

As Christians, we believe that you can only come to God through Jesus who is the way the truth and the life. We also believe that there is no other name by which we can be saved except the name of Jesus.

Because Satan is a cruel task master, he wants to attack God's creation and make sure that he takes as many of God's people as possible to hell. While he remains on this earth, his attack on mankind is a 'proxy war' that he wages against God himself. By tormenting people, he is hurting the heart of God even if these people are not born again. His mission is to steal, kill and destroy as much as possible in this proxy war.

He knows that those who do not have forgiveness for their sins will not enter heaven and he tries as much as possible to dangle a carrot of rest and relief while he knows quite well that he is simply harvesting souls for the punishment and torment of hell. If you die without Christ through suicide you are not going to heaven! Don't be fooled to take your life, because judgement awaits you!

"Whoever has the Son has life; whoever does not have God's Son does not have life." 1 John 5:12 NLT

"For Jesus is the one referred to in the Scriptures, where it says, 'The stone that you builders rejected has now become the cornerstone.' There is salvation in no one else! God has given no other name under heaven by which we must be saved."" Acts 4:12 NLT

THOSE WHO HAVE CHRIST

If you have Christ, you must be in a better position, right? I think not. I think it's a big gamble. There are several reasons for this. The Bible clearly tells us not to kill. Why? Because this is God's prerogative as he gives the gift of life and, with it, he assigns different life spans to different people.

Psalm 139 also says he has assigned a timeline for us to live in,

"And in Your book were all written the days that were appointed for me, when as yet there was not one of them [even taking shape]." Psalms 139:16 AMP

We cannot take it upon ourselves to cut short our lives as if we have the authority to do so. This is God's power and if God assigns us a certain number of days it is a sin to deliberately cut them short.

The damning consequences of 'deliberate sin' is also a reason why we should not commit suicide. The Bible warns against deliberate sin and says

"For if we go on willfully and deliberately sinning after receiving the knowledge of the truth, there no longer remains a sacrifice [to atone] for our sins [that is, no further offering to anticipate]," Hebrews 10:26 AMP

We are also reminded that we have a judgement and reward after this life, and we will answer and account for all our deeds

"For we [believers will be called to account and] must all appear before the judgment seat of Christ, so that each one may be repaid for what has been done in the body, whether good or bad [that is, each will be held responsible for his actions, purposes, goals, motives—the use or misuse of his time, opportunities and abilities]." 2 Corinthians 5:10 AMP

The outcome of willful sin is that we have no atonement or forgiveness for sin, and this is a dangerous gamble to make

"For if we go on willfully and deliberately sinning after receiving the knowledge of the truth, there no longer remains a sacrifice [to atone] for our sins [that is, no further offering to anticipate], but a kind of awful and terrifying expectation of [divine] judgment and THE FURY OF A FIRE and BURNING WRATH WHICH WILL CONSUME THE ADVERSARIES [those who put themselves in opposition to God]." Hebrews 10:26-27 AMP

PROVOKING GOD'S ANGER

The Bible seems to indicate that deliberate sin provokes the anger of God.

"How much greater punishment do you think he will deserve who

has rejected and trampled underfoot the Son of God, and has considered unclean and common the blood of the covenant that sanctified him, and has insulted the Spirit of grace [who imparts the unmerited favor and blessing of God]?" Hebrews 10:29 AMP

Why would suicide provoke God's anger? I think it's because, first of all, we are playing with the chance to life. We are also playing with the gift of salvation that God has given us through Jesus. Therefore, when we choose to take our life we literally despise and gamble with the saving work of Jesus on the cross. We choose to disobey one of the Ten Commandments which says, 'though shall not kill'.

A WASTE OF RESOURCES AND OPPORTUNITIES

We also waste all our achievements and the blessings of God in our lives. From the beginning we know that you and I have already overcome great odds in life. Mere conception though not taken seriously is a great feat of achievement. Though it takes just a single sperm to fertilize an egg you were that single sperm! And your competition was a swimming competition of about 100 million other swimmers.

In life God helps us overcome many odds, the stress of birth with or without complications, premature birth, infant mortality, illnesses at all ages, physical harm and attack, accidents, and so on. We also achieve great things in various levels of education or achieve recognition for workplace and other social and spiritual achievements. We earn diplomas and degrees, we use parent's or guardians' life savings to get an education, we get specialist training on the job or under and postgraduate and or vocational training using state and taxpayer resources in significant portions which all go as 'water down the drain'. How much money does it take to train a doctor or engineer or lawyer? How about an astronaut or a soldier and a special forces navy seal, or a policeman? Please don't waste this investment in yourself. It's unfair on your nation and on other taxpayers.

We start families and our spouses and families look up to and literally adore us. They have big hopes and dreams for the future, and beyond the family you are an emotional pillar for someone who looks up to you!

To throw all this away is not only sad but is truly a waste. It is such a waste that if done deliberately we have high chances of provoking God to anger!

As we have seen, God has a purpose for each and every one of us. In fact, his thoughts for us cannot be counted. When we 'throw in the towel' and deliberately 'kick the bucket', we equally frustrate the plans of God! Because while he has something planned for us, we deliberately stand against God, play God, pretend to own the breath of life and take our lives into our own hands.

12

Don't bury your coin

THIS IS THE CHALLENGE FROM GOD

There is a biblical example of provoking God by burying your coin. Remember the story of the ten talents? I bet you do; a master gave his servants coins or talents according to their abilities. To one he gave a single talent, but this dude simply buried his talent saying he did not do anything with it because he thought his master was a bad man.

How did the master react? With anger of course. The master has a bad impression and describes the lazy servant as not only wicked but slothful and lazy!

He said to him you should have invested the coin and done something worthwhile. He should have at least invested it in a bank.

I would like to submit to you that if this master represents God as we all believe it does, then God will have a similar reaction to us. Also, if God was angry with a coin that was not lost but was simply returned to him intact how much angrier will he be if we kill our lives and give it back to him empty? He will be very angry indeed!

ANGER AND BITTERNESS TOWARD GOD AND LIFE

Burying the coin is an act of bitterness. The servant said, "I knew you were a 'hard man'."

Haven't you heard this statement before? We sometimes think God is a hard man because of all the trials of life, and perhaps we think God does not love us, he is punishing us, or he simply brings suffering in the world and enjoys it. How can a good God allow suffering? We ask.

But this is a lie from the pit of hell! Suffering came because of sin and it comes because this is Satan's way of hurting the heart of God. God has put in place a redemption plan that first starts with receiving Jesus as Lord and savior and follows with the establishment of his kingdom on earth and restoring order.

Don't be bitter against God, his ways are not our ways. Also, he has given people free will and he does not force us to accept Jesus as our personal savior. He also follows his plan and timeframe of events, God is in no hurry to defeat the devil, he has already won the battle and will simply defeat the devil on the last day.

My simple illustration of the might and power of God is that on the last day God will not waist his energy to stand on his throne and enter into hand to hand combat with Satan, his mere creation, he will simply command an angel to bind him and throw him in the pit of hell. God is too powerful to dignify Satan with a mortal combat as if that were even possible! He would simply disintegrate in the mere presence of God. A single touch from God would annihilate him instantly.

"And then I saw an angel descending from heaven, holding the key of the abyss (the bottomless pit) and a great chain was in his hand. And he overpowered and laid hold of the dragon, that old serpent [of primeval times], who is the devil and Satan, and bound him [securely] for a thousand years (a millennium); and the angel hurled him into the abyss, and closed it and sealed it above him [preventing his escape or rescue], so that he would no longer deceive and seduce the nations, until the thousand years were at an end. After these things he must be liberated for a short time." Revelation 20 :1-3 AMP

"And the devil who had deceived them was hurled into the lake of fire and burning brimstone (sulfur), where the beast (Antichrist) and false prophet are also; and they will be tormented day and night, forever and ever." Revelation 20 :10 AMP

All I am saying here is that God is in control even though you and I think he is not. God can destroy the devil with a mere snap of his fingers, but he is too righteous to cheat, he will let things play themselves out with the rules he has set, and he will abide by them.

God plays the 'long game' and 'God will have the last laugh!' No doubt about that! So, don't be bitter with God, take bitterness away from your heart in the face of suffering.

The servant in the parable was so bitter that he did not want the Master to earn an income. This is the same mentality the enemy has. He does not want God to earn a return for his investment in your life!

He wants to waste the gift of your life and diminish it. Failing to earn an interest is failing to preserve the worth of anything. In finance there is a concept called 'time vale of money'. In layman's terms it means that, over time, the same amount of money loses value. That's why when you get a loan of $10,000 you don't just give it back the way you got it; you have to pay some interest to simply preserve its value. It also means the same $10,000 will not be able to buy the same value of goods in the future because things will have become expensive. To preserve its 'power to buy', you must add interest.

Friends, suicide is burying your coin in the ground with no return or gift for God. So please, please, please, don't bury your coin, don't be bitter against God, don't gamble with your destiny! Don't gamble with your eternity.

13

Putting your money in the bank

YOU ALWAYS HAVE AN ALTERNATIVE

If you think your life is worthless, or you don't have the ability to invest the talent of life that God has given you, then God is telling you to 'put your money in the bank!'

But what do we mean by 'putting your money' in the bank? Well, this largely means, simply preserving the value of your coin!

Preserving your coin, in my view means, two things.

Firstly, it means simply preserving your life. It means understanding that the coin you have was given to you! It's not yours. In fact, you are a steward of the 'coin of life' that God has given you. A steward is a mere agent of his master. And not the owner! As a steward you must preserve your coin of life.

Preserving your coin of life also implies 'simply fighting for' and 'holding on' to life. Sometimes you can't fight in your own strength, but you can at least hold on to God's hand,

"My soul [my life, my very self] clings to You; Your right hand upholds me." Psalms 63:8 AMP

David tells us a secret that 'when we cling to God, we are sustained and upheld by God's right hand!' Its an amazing revelation because though we are in a perilous situation we are lifted up and our feet do not slip

"The Lord makes firm the steps of the one who delights in him;" Psalms 37:23 NIV

"though he fall, he shall not be cast headlong,

for the LORD upholds his hand." Psalms 37:24 ESV

"though he may stumble, he will not fall, for the Lord upholds him with his hand." Psalms 37:24 NIV

The issue is that though you are in a dark situation, with things beyond your control or due to wrong decisions you have made in life, though you stumble, though you have fallen, the key to overcoming your odds is never to forsake God. Though things are dark you just need to 'hold on' to God don't fall into the trap of the devil which says, 'just free yourself and die'. That is a lie from the devil. He wants to harvest your soul into hell, he wants to kill your purpose in life.

The second meaning of putting your money in the bank is investing your life in things that are meaningful or are more productive than yourself despite the fact that your life or your investing abilities seem challenged or limited. It is a type of hunting for more fertile ground than your own.

Practically, I think this means 'investing in others' and I think this is something that all of us can do. When your life is not going on as planned, we should realize that we are not an island. Everyone, with very few exceptions, has someone looking up to them. This may be a relation, a child, friends or even people who are quietly encouraged by your life as they observe you from afar.

If you're like the gentleman who lost a spouse, you should know that there are kids who look up to you whose lives are fertile ground full of hope and expectation. If you don't have children, I say again, there are relations who are encouraged by your life and faith. If you want to kill yourself you can, instead, decide to live for these children, or decide to avoid traumatizing your relations with the shame and stigma of a suicidal death such as battling thoughts of what they could have done to avoid your suicide, and the pain of seeing you in a ghastly state after taking your own life.

If not for you, then you should do it for the love of those who love you and depend on you for support, whose life's will be destroyed due to your absence. You can do this even if you think your support is not adequate support. And indeed, because maybe your capabilities may have been affected and limited by the trauma you are in. Because at least, it can be emotional support that you can provide, the support of love, your very presence and availability, and the support of stability of mind. Just your love and affection are enough for your children and relations.

If you hold on and cling to God, he will again strengthen you, so you are not cast 'headlong', or 'completely flat' to the ground. He will not allow you to be completely destroyed, and if you are struggling with suicidal thoughts, he will help you overcome them. You will become like the gentleman my friend told me about, you will recover from your depression, you will wear a smile on your face, and you will want to live life again.

You will appreciate this decision when you look at the joy on your children's face, when you feel the energy in their laugh and the warmth of their hug, and when you see the sparkle in their eyes as they believe that all things are now possible just because they have you around. The same goes for your family, your siblings, friends and relatives. Just imagine, if these get a sparkle in their eyes, and yet they don't know what good things God has in store for you, how much more do you think God rejoices when you choose to live? How excited is he when he looks at all the plans, he has for you to fulfill?

But you might say, 'I have no one' or 'nobody loves me'. That may be slightly true but remember that sometimes God's purposes are beyond you and sometimes it's about your children and God wants you to ensure that you live so your children can accomplish their heavenly assignment. What if Naomi committed suicide after losing not only her husband but her two sons as well? It means Ruth's purpose of being a wife to Boaz and of being one of the great great grandmothers of Jesus would not have been fulfilled.

So, the moment you take your life you are frustrating God's plan, and this should not happen.

And, what we learn from this parable of the ten talents is that killing yourself is not the easy way out. Quite the contrary, it is the traumatic way out. It is a way out that is fueled and filled with the deceit and lies of the devil. It is actually a further affliction of pain on those who love and surround you.

It is an abortion of purpose, not only for you but also for future generations, it's an abortion that must not be allowed.

Most of all, it looks to me it is an act of defiance. a defiant act of assumed ownership of your soul. An act of defiance of being the captain of your own soul and burying your coin in bitterness. A defiant act of not wanting your master to see any good benefit from your life and above all, a selfish act of not even thinking about those who love and support you. You don't just kill yourself; you kill the spirits and dignity of your whole family too!

CHOOSING NOT TO BE DECEIVED

As far as taking our own lives is concerned, we need to choose who to believe between God's word and the voice of frustration that comes from the pit of hell. Because by nature, Satan is firstly a murderer and a liar and he actually wants to do both these things to you, lie to and ultimately clobber and murder or terminate you.

He was a murderer from the beginning, and does not stand in the truth, because there is no truth in him. When he lies, he speaks out of his own character, for he is a liar and the father of lies (John 8:44).

The fact that Satan tells all these lies to those who commit suicide means he is simply blinding them in order to terminate their life and purpose.

He is lying that they will get an escape and rest when, quite to the contrary, he wants to murder them in line with his nature and see them anger God.

He also wants to ensure that they suffer the judgement of

God for 'deliberate sin' for which there is no atonement. He also wants to anger God and Jesus their master and maker who will judge and describe them as, not only selfish, but wicked.

As to the outcome, there is something we see in the parable. Jesus said this bitter servant should be thrown to the outer darkness where there is weeping and gnashing of teeth.

"So, take the talent from him and give it to him who has the ten talents. And cast the worthless servant into the outer darkness. In that place there will be weeping and gnashing of teeth." Matthew 25:28-30 ESV

I would like to submit to you that taking your life is open defiance before God, it's taking a gamble at angering and disappointing God. It's about standing up to God and playing God in his place, it is risking being thrown out of God's kingdom, about aborting God's purposes and deliberately inciting God to anger. It is staring God's judgement in the face.

When you take your life, you should imagine demons waiting with their long and evil claws to shackle and drag you into the dark and fiery pits of hell!

HOW I PUT MY MONEY IN THE BANK

When I was thinking about these principles, I thought it worthwhile to share how I also put my money in the bank in my dark season. After a string of losses of loved ones, from my sister, to my wife to my dad, you can experience an emotional assault on many fronts. A sister's loss brings emotions of what else you could have done to save her. Depending on who you are, you will have your own frustrations, as a parent who is a nurturer and protector, as a big brother who protects the princes and princesses of the family, or a sibling who looks out for her with similar love, affection and protection to your princess and sibling.

The loss of a wife turns your life upside down, literally. Life changes for you and your children and also for your family at large! Your daily routine, changes, you sense a gap, the depths of which are unknown until you start living again and you try to fill those deceptively big shoes. And even if you do, there are things you can simply never achieve!

The death of a father leads children to think they have failed miserably in supporting and protecting their dad. Questions remain unanswered of what they ought to have done better. How things have been missed for a very long time or right under their noses.

All these emotions are not easy to process. You run the risk of being overcome by depression and crushing grief. Personally, I felt it has put me in a state of mental chaos in which you can't really process much. You don't know what the future holds, or how to live energetically and enthusiastically. You actually feel numb most of the time, and sometimes not fully aware or awake, or not fully alive. You feel something, a big chunk of you is missing.

In the midst of all this chaos, in the midst of this emotional storm, there are some things I decided to continue doing after my wife Debbie died. One of them is just getting back to work after I had recovered from my injuries. I tried not to get buried into it too much to allow for a balance and the processing of my emotions as well.

I later returned to church and though it was hard, I processed those emotions too. I continued to help out in church in the areas I was involved in before and this helped me get my structure and routine back, also it helped me make positive contributions in the lives of others that surrounded me.

Most of all, my kids were the center of my world. I was encouraged to do my best for them, because they take confidence in me also. I have to ensure that I do right by them in the best way possible. So I continue holding on to my faith and sharing my faith with my children so they don't despair on the demise of their mother but remain hopeful that not only is she in God's presence, but also that they will meet her alive in heaven one day, and, finally, that our God will take care of us here on earth!

The fact that I am there with them also helps them gain confidence that it's going to be all right. We all don't know how, but we are thankful that we have each other, in this way we live and remain hopeful, a day at a time! Just a day at a time, and we are grateful for each new day!

14

Overcoming suicide and suicidal thoughts

There are several practical steps that can be taken to overcome suicide and suicidal thoughts which we explore below.

GETTING HELP AND OPENING UP

The higher rate of suicide in men as compared to women is no accident or statistical anomaly. It ranges from about twice to four times the rate of women from country to country. This high rate occurs because men are generally less expressive than women. They choose to suffer alone because society has boxed them up into a prison corner of stigma and cultural expectations.

Society says, 'men don't cry', and so they don't cry when the carry burden after burden of trauma, until a single straw breaks their backs one day.

They have been told to 'be a man!' To be macho and at times to be selfish and show their manhood by inappropriate habits of substance abuse and sexual exploits which might have landed them in mentally stressful situations in the first place.

We must all choose to get help and get counseling if need be. I remember I was given the opportunity to utilize my employer's wellness program through my own loss of my wife. It helped get a lot of perspective on things and help me process my own pain. So, don't think that counseling is for those who have mental illness alone, it's also for those who simply have stressful situations that they are going through and are trying to manage.

I used to joke with friends of mine that I am going to see the doctor for mad people, they would ask are you mad and I would say, 'I think so'. But I did it and stuck to my sessions anyway.

This is especially difficult for those who get caught up in sins or other failures in society and the corporate world, such as financial scandals or behavioral and performance matters.

Even in challenging marriage or relationship situations we can reach out for help, and to overcome the stigma that 'we are fighting or failing to run our marriage or relationship smoothly'.

We need to find a mature person who can help us while maintaining our dignity in the church, workplace or society in general. Suffering in silence is unhealthy and must be avoided at all costs.

FINANCIAL PRUDENCE AND WISDOM

It is clear that we ought to avoid decisions that can put us into overbearing debt. We need to assess our financial muscle and live within our means and not go with the flow of society. Let's avoid living by trends and start focusing on what works for us as a person, a couple or a family. You are running your own race and there is no need to compete with others. People with different destinations in life can't really compete because they are going to different places and mostly in different directions.

If you can avoid loan sharks that will do you a lot of good. If you don't, you may end up committing crimes to support your lifestyle and living a corrupt life that is not in tandem with your values and faith or the ethics of your workplace.

Other financial burdens are gambling and impulse buying, sometimes we need to tame our decisions in this regard, so we don't overstretch our limits. Gambling can be addictive and it may require that we get more specific help in this area too especially if it is wasting our resources, setting our priorities upside down or compromising our quality of life and that of our immediate family and of those around us.

DON'T LOSE YOUR MIND

Not losing our minds is about taking a lot of mental action to direct and channel our thoughts so that we don't succumb to acutely depressing and potentially suicidal thoughts.

The Bible says, 'as a man thinks in his heart so is he' Proverbs 23:7. This means we must not allow negativity to fill us and fuel our thoughts because these thoughts may overtake us and lead to feelings of hopelessness and worthlessness. These should not be allowed to take root in our minds.

Based on the discussions in this book, you can begin by believing with me that God has a purpose for you and also for those around you, and if not those around you then even your children and their children. You have to quieten the lies of the devil and learn from the stories we discussed regarding how people in the Bible managed to overcome their challenges.

We must choose to believe that we will see God's goodness in the land of the living! We must hold on to hope and if all else fails, to simply cling to God!

"Finally, believers, whatever is true, whatever is honorable and worthy of respect, whatever is right and confirmed by God's word, whatever is pure and wholesome, whatever is lovely and brings peace, whatever is admirable and of good repute; if there is any excellence, if there is anything worthy of praise, think continually on these things [center your mind on them, and implant them in your heart]." Philippians 4:8 AMP

MIND YOUR LANGUAGE

We need to mind what we say. This is because thoughts and speech have a cyclical relationship. They feed on each other. The more you think about something the more you speak it. And the more you speak it then the more you think it.

The Bible in Luke 6:45: says 'out of the abundance of your heart the mouth speaks'. This is why you must deliberately create a positive 'word and speech cycle'.

If there is a mismatch in either one, you disturb the positive cycle and compromise whatever positive effort and attribute remains. If you have good thoughts your negative speech will plant negative seeds in your mind, and you will start thinking negative thoughts. If your thoughts are bad, you will no longer have the conviction in your speech, and it will no longer remain wholesome and positive. So, watch your cycle and create a positive 'speech and thought cycle' deliberately and at all times.

Create good treasure in your heart by thinking about good thinks and hoping for good things and it will bubble up into positive speech

"You brood of vipers; how can you speak good things when you are evil? For the mouth speaks out of that which fills the heart. The good man, from his [inner] good treasure, brings out good things; and the evil man, from his [inner] evil treasure, brings out evil things." Matthew 12:34-35 AMP

"A good person produces good things from the treasury of a good heart, and an evil person produces evil things from the treasury of an evil heart. What you say flows from what is in your heart." Luke 6:45 NLT

These verses emphasize that when you are evil, you can't speak good things and that we need to fill our hearts with the treasure of good thoughts.

If you hear someone say he will kill himself, never take it lightly because their hearts are already filled with suicidal thoughts. We should not discount them because we think they are drunk or irresponsible, immature or irrational, because it's actually a sign of trouble and sometimes a mischievous and hidden cry for help. We must approach them with love and help them.

PRAYER

The life of David is one filled with persecution from his enemies but at the same time it is also filled with prayers and reaching out to God. Prayer is powerful and is required by both the distressed and those who support them. We should all stand in prayer together. In fact, when we pray, we demonstrate our realization that this is actually a spiritual battle. Especially in people who have battled for so long and are bordering on psychotic and mental pressures and illnesses. It becomes more evident that this is a spiritual battle when they start 'losing their minds'.

"For our struggle is not against flesh and blood [contending only with physical opponents], but against the rulers, against the powers, against the world forces of this [present] darkness, against the spiritual forces of wickedness in the heavenly (supernatural) places." Ephesians 6:12 AMP

When we realize this, we can pray and stand in the gap for them and we can pray against premature death,

"He protects them from the grave, from crossing over the river of death." Job 33:18 NLT

"They lose their appetite for even the most delicious food. Their flesh wastes away, and their bones stick out. They are at death's door; the angels of death wait for them. "But if an angel from heaven appears— a special messenger to intercede for a person and declare that he is upright— he will be gracious and say, 'Rescue him from the grave, for I have found a ransom for his life.' Then his body will become as healthy as a child's, firm and youthful again." Job 33:20-25 NLT

This passage talks of people who are physically weak and are battling with sickness, those who are wasting away, and are at death's door, and even angels of death are ready to take them, these symptoms are also felt by those who are fighting bouts of depression like the gentleman that my friend Dharles helped.

God says if someone is found to play the role of an angel or a 'God send' or 'messenger of God' or simply put, 'an intercessor' God will save that person's life!' You can be that angel; you can be that intercessor!

So, whenever you stand in the gap for someone firstly be available, because *'only 1 among a thousand is enough to move the hand of God!'*

God does not always use an army of intercessors. He only needs one, just one among a thousand people! So, next time you are urged in your heart to pray for someone just be available as a vessel that God can use. Even if you are that single vessel. One vessel is enough! You are enough!

"But if an angel from heaven appears— a special messenger to intercede for a person and declare that he is upright— he will be gracious'

When you are available to stand in the gap you become that messenger and that angel. It's not that a physical angel will always come down, but you will be an 'extension of God's kingdom' and become that angel, you become a life saver and you become that intercessor!

Secondly, we need to declare them as righteous by the ransom that was already paid on their behalf

"But if an angel from heaven appears— a special messenger to intercede for a person and ***declare that he is righteous****"*

I am reminded of the Israelites in Egypt who were protected from the plague of the death of the first born. They were told to sprinkle blood on their door posts and the angel of death did not come to their houses. The same principle applies. The blood of the lamb in Egypt speaks of the blood of Jesus which is a ransom for the sins of the world. If we pray for someone, we should pray for the covering of the blood of Jesus upon them and therefore we should declare them forgiven and ransomed by this blood!

When God hears your prayer, he will be gracious and give the command, '*Rescue him from the grave, for I have found a ransom for his life.*'

Once the command is given our life is protected and our health is restored.

Finally, we should stand in the gap boldly and audaciously, knowing that God is able. We should also stand in the gap constantly and frequently. This is in keeping with the revelation that God is actually in the business of saving people from premature death! Why is this the case? Because premature deaths slow down the advancement of God's kingdom. As seen in the lives of Jesus and Moses, all of them would have had their purposes terminated had they been killed in infancy. Likewise, if we die before achieving our purposes in life, the purpose of God is aborted before it's time and denied the opportunity to bless his creation! Premature death is so evil for this reason and so, God's business is to ensure that time and time again he delivers his people from this evil and this abomination!

""Yes, God does these things again and again for people. He rescues them from the grave so they may enjoy the light of life."

Job 33:29-30 NLT

Some versions of the Bible say God does this '*twice and even three times*' but this translation puts it well and sheds more light. God does this '*again and again*' meaning that he does it, *contin-*

ually, whenever there is need and without limit!' Simply put .... *'it's God's business to deliver from premature death!'*

So, if it's God's business....

why not pray boldly?

why not pray audaciously?

why not pray arrogantly and continuously for God to deliver?

Why not declare and say 'I will pray, I will be among the one in a thousand as often as God moves me to do so! God being my help!'

DON'T FIND SOLACE IN SUBSTANCES!

The biggest mistake we can make in dark times is to run to substances like alcohol or other substances like tobacco and related drugs.

It's a slow fade to give your mind and morals away. It starts with a glass of alcohol or wine, because it's the naturally available solace when you are all alone. And soon you need to consume more than you normally do or can handle until you just need one more, and then one more, and then one more. Your behavior begins to change, your life starts getting affected as you miss and can no longer give attention to important things, you start making bad decisions and later you can't escape the clutches of the substances you are abusing. You start failing to manage your budget, getting into other vices like immorality and prostitution and similar evils all because you took solace in the wrong things.

So, even if you normally take alcohol according to your personal beliefs or your faith, it is advisable not to run to it in difficult times lest, in your desperation, you get caught in its clutches.

INVESTMENTS IN MENTAL HEALTH SERVICES

On a larger scale, it is important for governments, organizations, churches and societies to make efforts to invest in mental health services. Some churches have structures for HIV services, and I think it is possible to extend this to mental wellness in general. It may not be possible to hire trained psychologists immediately, or at all, but it is possible to cover the basics in a training module for existing staff.

Governments should make similar investments and bring mental health services to the citizens.

All these organizations should ensure that they fight the stigma of getting help and especially the stigma against men who seek this help.

For church and society, they should make sure to help their own and not condemn or sideline them. Once people who have erred or sinned in the church know they will be faced with judgement and not grace, they will choose to suffer and nurse their wounds in silence. Unfortunately for most, their wounds will become septic and they will die alone in a deep sense of guilt, shame and rejection. The church is one of the organizations that is very good at shooting its own and at simply ignoring and avoiding them in segregation and condemnation. This should not be the case!

15

Perceiving and breaking the curse of suicide

Suicide is just as spiritual a matter as a demonic assault on our souls. In fact, it ultimately manifests itself as a spirit. Ordinarily, destructive angels of death exist, but these spirits of death, that come from the pit of hell, at times specialize in attacking people with suicide.

Another way they assault us is by bringing a curse of suicide. When this happens suicide will usually manifest in a continuous generational cycle.

While not all suicide is from an ancestral curse, there are others that are clearly generational and ancestral. For example, there are some families whose history will be riddled with suicide every now and again and perhaps more than 2 or 3 people will commit suicide in a single generation. And the same will apply in the next generation and so on and so on.

At this point, we need discernment to perceive that there is indeed a pattern of assault and repetition and a need to start working towards breaking that cycle.

"For our struggle is not against flesh and blood [contending only with physical opponents], but against the rulers, against the powers, against the world forces of this [present] darkness, against the spiritual forces of wickedness in the heavenly (supernatural) places." Ephesians 6:12 AMP

Once we realize that suicide is spiritual, and premature death in general is a spiritual attack we need to use weapons that are effective in the spiritual dimension too. It is only spiritual weapons that are 'divinely powerful' to destroy such fortresses and fortified powers.

"For though we walk in the flesh [as mortal men], we are not carrying on our [spiritual] warfare according to the flesh and using the weapons of man. The weapons of our warfare are not physical [weapons of flesh and blood]. Our weapons are divinely powerful for the destruction of fortresses." 2 Corinthians 10:3-4 AMP

The key message is, *'we might be in the flesh, a suicide may seemingly have a logical reason but please open your eyes and see that this is a spiritual matter and that premature death is always spiritual warfare!'*

TRIGGERS OF CURSES

Curses usually have a trigger. In fact, it is not possible for a curse to settle on you if there is no trigger, reason or cause,

"Like the sparrow in her wandering, like the swallow in her flying, So the curse without cause does not come and alight [on the undeserving]." Proverbs 26:2 AMP

Generally, curses are earned or triggered, and we see this in the story of Abel who was killed by his brother. Once he was killed, Cain was cursed by God.

"And now you are cursed from the ground, which has opened its mouth to receive your brother's [shed] blood from your hand." Genesis 4:11 AMP

In the case of Judas, you could say that he was operating under a curse. He had effectively shed the blood of Jesus and was under the assault and darkness of the spirit of death. That is why we need to pray against premature death and include people who have committed grave sins. When people commit sin, Satan, who is by nature the accuser of the brethren, brings curses and accusations and blinds people from seeing the love and mercy of God. They are finally tormented in their spirits and struck down by Satan in his quest to slow down the advancement of the kingdom of God, cutting short dreams and aborting God's purposes.

The second trigger of suicide is the sins of our fathers. God speaks of himself as not only a jealous God but one who visits the sins of fathers to the third and fourth generations.

"You shall not worship them nor serve them; for I, the LORD your God, am a jealous (impassioned) God [demanding what is rightfully and uniquely mine], visiting (avenging) the iniquity (sin, guilt) of the fathers on the children [that is, calling the children to account for the sins of their fathers], to the third and fourth generations of those who hate Me, but showing graciousness and steadfast lovingkindness

to thousands [of generations] of those who love Me and keep My commandments." Exodus 20:5-6 AMP

This simply means sometimes there are things that may have occurred in the past that are opening a door to the spirit of suicide but of which we know nothing about. This is a problem and perhaps that's why we see some tragedies continually happening in some families.

We will proceed to discuss how to break the curse of suicide.

CONFESSING ANCESTRAL SINS

An interesting question was posed by some Israelites who were told in judgement that they would be taken into captivity. The question was 'why, what have we done wrong to deserve this?'

God gave two simple but valid and crystal-clear reasons. First, because of their fathers' sin and secondly, because of their own sin.

""Now when you tell these people all these words and they ask you, 'Why has the LORD decreed all this great tragedy against us? And what is our iniquity, what is the sin which we have committed against the LORD our God?' Then you are to say to them, 'It is because your fathers have abandoned (rejected) Me,' says the LORD, 'and have walked after other gods and have served them and bowed down to the handmade idols and have abandoned (rejected) Me and have not kept My law," Jeremiah 16:10-11 AMP

This was the sin of their fathers, but their own sin was in the following scripture

"and because you have done worse [things] than your fathers. Just

look, every one of you walks in the stubbornness of his own evil heart, so that you do not listen [obediently] to Me." Jeremiah 16:12 AMP

When judgement fell on Israel the same prophet Jeremiah now said,

"Our fathers sinned and are no more; It is we who have carried their sin." Lamentations 5:7 AMP

We need to confess the sin of our fathers because something spiritual happens when people sin and wrong others. There are always tears that were shed and hearts that were broken. These hearts and these tears cry out to God and sometimes curses may have been pronounced that give authority to the devil to torment you as a way of bringing and executing justice. This was the case with Abel whose blood cried out to God and also for David who prayed dangerous prayers of God's vindication against his enemies.

"The LORD said, "What have you done? The voice of your brother's [innocent] blood is crying out to Me from the ground [for justice]." Genesis 4:10 AMP

David on the other hand summoned God to attack his enemy and in Psalm 109 he prays a prayer that is believed to be a prophecy against Judas who would betray Jesus,

"O God of my praise! Do not keep silent, For the mouth of the wicked and the mouth of the deceitful are opened against me; They have spoken against me with a lying tongue. They have also surrounded me with words of hatred and have fought against me without a cause. In return for my love, they attack me, But I am in prayer. They have repaid me evil for good, And hatred for my love. Appoint a wicked man against him, and let an attacker stand at his right hand [to kill him]." Psalms 109:1-6 AMP

When we look at this passage, and this is only part of the whole chapter, we start to understand that Judas was indeed under the assault of a curse and therefore, even if we don't know the sins of our fathers, we ought to confess them and ask for forgiveness.

"We know and acknowledge, O LORD, our wickedness and the iniquity of our fathers; for we have sinned against You. Do not treat us with contempt and condemn us, for Your own name's sake; Do not disgrace Your glorious throne; Remember [with consideration] and do not break Your [solemn] covenant with us." Jeremiah 14:20-21 AMP

In addition to this we need to confess the current sins of our families so we can start breaking the power of the curse.

""O Lord our God, you brought lasting honor to your name by rescuing your people from Egypt in a great display of power. But we have sinned and are full of wickedness. In view of all your faithful mercies, Lord, please turn your furious anger away from your city Jerusalem, your holy mountain. All the neighboring nations mock Jerusalem and your people because of our sins and the sins of our ancestors. "O our God, hear your servant's prayer! Listen as I plead. For your own sake, Lord, smile again on your desolate sanctuary. "O my God, lean down and listen to me. Open your eyes and see our despair. See how your city—the city that bears your name—lies in ruins. We make this plea, not because we deserve help, but because of your mercy. "O Lord, hear. O Lord, forgive. O Lord, listen and act! For your own sake, do not delay, O my God, for your people and your city bear your name."" Daniel 9:15-19 NLT

THE CROSS OF JESUS

The cross of Jesus is extremely powerful in breaking not only the curse but all other powers of the enemy! It is a place where firstly we get salvation and secondly, where all powers of the devil are defeated.

When we are not in Jesus Christ, the devil has a legal claim and charge on our lives, but the cross of Jesus cancels that legal claim so that the devil can no longer 'press charges' against you before God.

"You were dead because of your sins and because your sinful nature was not yet cut away. Then God made you alive with Christ, for he forgave all our sins. He canceled the record of the charges against us and took it away by nailing it to the cross. In this way, he disarmed the spiritual rulers and authorities. He shamed them publicly by his victory over them on the cross." Colossians 2:13-15 NLT

What Paul is emphasizing here is that the power of the cross can only be appropriated or applied to our lives by receiving Jesus as Lord and Savior and 'being made alive' in Jesus as opposed to being 'dead in your sins'.

Secondly, Jesus' death was specifically tailored to break all curses on your life. While charges range from sins to curses, he did something that is specifically targeted at breaking the curse.

"But those who depend on the law to make them right with God are under his curse, for the Scriptures say, "Cursed is everyone who does not observe and obey all the commands that are written in God's Book of the Law."

But Christ has rescued us from the curse pronounced by the law. When he was hung on the cross, he took upon himself the curse for our wrongdoing. For it is written in the Scriptures, "Cursed is everyone who is hung on a tree."" Galatians 3:10, 13 NLT

The good news we have is that Jesus himself carried our curse. He actually became cursed on our behalf. That's why on the day he was crucified, there was darkness on the face of the earth. The darkness came because Jesus 'became and carried' our sin and had to face abandonment or separation from God! That's why he cried 'My God, my God why have you forsaken me!' It as this point that he became cursed because the Old Testament law says cursed is everyone who hangs on a tree.

We can therefore see that without Jesus in our lives we are at certain risk of suffering from ancestral curses of all types. And, deliverance from curses starts with giving your life to Jesus otherwise you have no defense or any weapon with which to wage this spiritual war.

THE BLOOD OF JESUS

The blood of Jesus is another powerful weapon at our disposal. The blood completely counters the quest for vengeance by people and even the devil. While we saw that the blood of Abel was crying out to God for vengeance and justice, and while the devil wants to lay a legal charge on us, this blood speaks of better things. Instead of vengeance and judgement the blood of Jesus cries for mercy. It says, 'the debt is paid', and 'all charges are cancelled'.

This blood is the same blood that rebuked the angel of death that killed the firstborn sons in Egypt and brought the covering of God's presence over the households of the Israelites.

"You have come to Jesus, the one who mediates the new covenant between God and people, and to the sprinkled blood, which speaks of forgiveness instead of crying out for vengeance like the blood of Abel." Hebrews 12:24 NLT

"and to Jesus, the Mediator of a new covenant [uniting God and man], and to the sprinkled blood, which speaks [of mercy], a better and nobler and more gracious message than the blood of Abel [which cried out for vengeance]." Hebrews 12:24 AMP

The blood of Jesus must be pleaded and sprinkled over our families so as to break the power of any curses that may come from our forefathers. If we are parents, we must pray over our children and plead the blood of Jesus to work in their lives. If there is someone who is struggling with suicidal thoughts and statements, we should also wage spiritual warfare and break the power of any curses through the blood of Jesus.

This blood is the atonement that can be their ransom for the curse and can literally save their lives, and even if someone is not a believer you can pray on their behalf and allow God to deliver them,

""If there is an angel as a mediator for him, One out of a thousand, To explain to a man what is right for him [that is, how to be in right standing with God], Then the angel is gracious to him, and says, 'Spare him from going down to the pit [of destruction]; I have found a ransom [a consideration, or reason for redemption, an atonement]!'" Job 33:23-24 AMP

"And they overcame him by the blood of the Lamb, and by the word of their testimony." Revelation 12 :11 KJV

Friends... it is time to overcome by the blood of Jesus!

THE ANOINTING

"And it shall come to pass in that day, that his burden shall be taken away from off thy shoulder, and his yoke from off thy neck, and the yoke shall be destroyed because of the anointing." Isaiah 10:27 KJV

The anointing speaks of the power of the Holy Spirit in our lives. In Isaiah there is a promise that the yoke will be broken because of the anointing. The anointing empowers the agenda of God's kingdom. Jesus announced his divine, noble and outstanding purpose and the supernatural power behind it when he read the scroll in the synagogue and announced that the Spirit of the Lord was upon him and the purpose was clear, to proclaim liberty to the captives! Jesus came to set the captives free even the captives of suicide.

"For this purpose the Son of God was manifested, that he might destroy the works of the devil." 1 John 3:8 KJV

"The Spirit of the Lord is upon me, because he hath anointed me to preach the gospel to the poor; he hath sent me to heal the brokenhearted, to preach deliverance to the captives, and recovering of sight to the blind, to set at liberty them that are bruised, To preach the acceptable year of the Lord." Luke 4:18-19 KJV

Therefore, we should always pray that the anointing of God's Holy Spirit should rest upon our families and individually on us as well.

There are few other things that help break or keep curses at bay. Including mere obedience as indicated in Deuteronomy 28, which is a chapter that talks of obedience and blessings and also disobedience and curses. However, I feel that the ones mentioned above are most applicable for the specific suicidal curse that is in question here.

So, if you are to benefit from this discussion, we should ensure we have Jesus in our heart as Lord and deliberately confess all known and unknown sin of our fathers and those of our families like Daniel did. We should break the curse by claiming the triumphant power of the cross that breaks every curse. We should, lastly, stand in the gap for others by pleading the blood of Jesus and calling and invoking the anointing on those that need our prayer.

May God give you the victory over the curse of suicide and all other curses as you apply these principles in the name of Jesus!

16

The conclusion of the matter

WHERE OUR LOVED ONES GO

As you can see, the Bible does not deal with the issue of suicide directly. We do however see from God's word that deciding to take your life is a big deal with big risks for eternity. It would seem this is especially true for those whose faculties are intact.

For others however we see that they may not have full cognitive capabilities to decide to avoid suicide. For this group of people, I would like to remind you that I see them as wounded soldiers, or those that are killed in action.

Their souls are relentlessly assaulted, and they fall prey to the enemy. But who are we to judge another man's servant?

"Who are you to condemn someone else's servants? Their own mas-

ter will judge whether they stand or fall. And with the Lord's help, they will stand and receive his approval." Romans 14:4 NLT

I think what God wants us to know is that he has given us, as children of God, a clear warning. I also think the word is clear regarding what to expect when we die without Christ or the risk we bear when we take our own lives. And, we must be touched just as God's heart is touched when people succumb to the assault of their souls.

Lastly, we should all do our part to 'carry and protect our wounded' who struggle or are slain in battle. We should pray and be used by God to stand in the gap! Considering the mercy of God, let's not be surprised if we find that some of the slain are in heaven. Because with the Lord's help we can stand and be accepted by God! Oh yes, it's possible with this merciful and loving God. But it's his prerogative alone!

God wants us to know that the secret things belong to God! What we know, even though little is to help us worship him and heed his word. So, don't gamble with life but be filled with compassion for those who fall in battle. Better yet, use the knowledge God has equipped you to strengthen those who would otherwise be slain in battle!

FINAL THOUGHTS

An abortion of the unborn is sad enough but an abortion of the already born is an evil that is mercilessly devastating. It is a hope deferred that indeed makes the heart sick, not just for the victims but even the affected and this is an evil that must not persist. It is a battle tactic that is born from the very pit of hell.

In an attempt to impede the advancement of God's kingdom, the enemy must slow it down as much as he can. He will therefore try to destroy all potential foot soldiers and nip them in the bud when they are still in the womb and are most vulnerable. If he fails, this tactic he will ambush them with a brutal assault of the mind and soul to the point that they desert the army of God in which they have enlisted or before they get a chance to enlist. This strategy is a sinister and diabolical art of war. But unfortunately, it's a strategy the enemy has used for millennia and we must respond and respond we will. With prayer, with knowledge and with support to the wounded amongst us!

17

Common causes of suicide

Our World in Data and the World Health Organization identify various causes and risk factors that lead to suicide which we shall briefly discuss.

FINANCES

Financial problems have been known to lead to suicide. Sometimes too much debt can lead to a crushing burden that results in inability to service repayments and in eventual loss of various personal property. Some people have been known to fail to tame their appetite for debt and have found themselves caught up in its clutches.

Others have also swam in the dangerous waters of loan

sharks. Loan sharks are what they are.... *'sharks that devour their prey'*. Countless stories are told of well-respected professionals in society who swam in these waters. They borrow a loan of $1,000 in their currency equivalent and mean to repay on a certain date, but the loan shark disappears on payment date. All his associates simply say he was here but is nowhere to be seen, his phones can't be reached, if he has an office it is closed or the people can't serve you because he is not there and before you know it you have missed the deadline!

The very next day or two you receive harassing calls of why you did not repay, and you are told your loan is now $2,000. The trend continues until before you know it your loan is $20,000. You are now properly cornered! At this point you are constantly harassed and threatened with loss of property such as vehicles and even houses.

You are now in their clutches and may even be pulled into a life of crime as repayment for their debt, especially if they are into criminal activities. I know of someone who fled his country, leaving his young family of a wife and children, on account of such ruthless loan sharks. Others I know or heard of have lost property, live in hiding, have been forced to steal to repay huge debts and some have, sadly, succumbed to the pressure and have literally taken their own life. When you hear of loan shark chronicles the stories sound like fiction coming straight from a movie but unfortunately, they are eerily true.

FAILURE

Failure of different kinds has led some to believe that the easiest way out is suicide. Many people who have failed in business have had significant financial negative consequences leading to desperation and a feeling of low self-worth.

Others have failed academically after exerting so much effort. Others have failed to get the political or professional appointment or promotion they hoped for. Perhaps it has been denied from them and this is seen as a form of failure. Depending on personal pride, culture or social pressure this has led some to take their own lives.

ABUSE

Bullying and harassment and other forms of abuse including gender-based violence have also led to people feeling completely worthless. This abuse can be not only physical, but also verbal and emotional.

GUILT AND SHAME

Guilt and shame are really a broad term and can be caused by many things. While these emotions arise from all failures in general, I want to relate them more to moral failures and sins.

Recently, there was a suicide of man who slept with his wife's niece who was living with them. Once found out by his wife he apologized and sought forgiveness. The wife agreed to forgive him but wanted her niece to return to her home with the promise that they would continue to financially support her even though she would no longer live in their home.

The husband found himself in a dilemma because he wondered how they would explain themselves when returning their niece to her home. The wife said they will find something to say but the husband knew that the cat would eventually come out of the bag!

The wife insisted and took the niece home but, on her return, found that her husband had taken his own life, dangling from the ceiling. She was stunned! She was devastated.

Her husband was deeply prayerful and feared that once this news was out, he would be expelled from their faith community. Considering his status in society he would also experience endless shame, as he pictured it!

The wife blamed herself endlessly for this and wondered what else she should have done and how else she should have compromised to save both her marriage and her husband at the same time.

She knew her husband was remorseful and genuinely sought forgiveness, she knew he was a mentally stable husband and that he was ordinarily very faithful to her and that the sexual immorality was uncharacteristic of him. He was a good husband after all, had she pushed him too far? She thought to herself.

This story is only one of many versions of similar stories of people who commit incest by sleeping with their children or parents or siblings for whatever reason. It is the same variant that manifests in cases of infidelity when well-meaning people fall into sin and are covered in the muddy guilt and shame that is visible for all to see.

Others fall victim to rape or being the rapists. They all battle with these feelings of guilt and shame. They battle feelings of discrimination and unimportance as a husband or wife who is no longer desirable for marriage or is no longer a virgin because of the rape and abuse. The shame and stigma can overpower and lead someone to think of taking their own life.

Another devastating form of failure is broken relationships and divorce. All these can lead to deep emotion.

DEATH

Death is very very complex because every situation is unique, and its impact is equally different. The death of a child at both a young and older age is a shattering of hopes and dreams for both the parents and family.

The death of parents can lead children and dependents vulnerable to financial exposure, need and poverty. Especially if they are not yet financially independent.

The death of a sibling can lead to great loss of companionship and camaraderie, sometimes it leads to a financial gap that may not be easily filled especially if they were instrumental in providing support.

The death of a spouse is equally damaging from many fronts, taking on double responsibility, loneliness and general feelings of despair. In all these situations the gap is real, and the emotional and financial toll can be significant and the psychological dent enormous!

My friend Dharles, as she was checking up on and encouraging me in my own loss, told me a story of someone she randomly met at a shopping mall. She first saw a lost, or almost lost child, who was wandering all alone. Asking the child where his parents were, he answered, almost fearfully, and later pointed to his daddy.

She took him back and lamented that the child could have been run over or abducted but the daddy couldn't care less. Looking unkempt, stressed and physically depressed, she wondered at his callous response and probed him further as to why this happened and what was going on in his life.

He wondered why she was not minding her own business but if you know Dharles, bubbly, bold and driven, she pressed on and was determined to get to the bottom of this. There was no escaping her now.

She discovered the man had lost his wife recently and he saw no point of living. He was oblivious to the fact that his children need and look up to him. She told him that he has a purpose to live for and that though he does not feel like it he has his two little children who need him. His children lost their mommy but should not lose their daddy too. It's painful for the kids to see their daddy give up on life and give up on them too as if they are worthless and not worth living and fighting for. Dharles told him 'I want to keep tabs on you' and since she lived in another city, she linked him up with someone who himself had experienced loss. She was checking up on him together with her contact.

He was a true picture of chronic depression. He lamented that he could not sleep, he was angry at his wife's death, he had no spark or interest to do anything. Not even to work or eat or be around friends, looking at him he was now rather skinny and had lost weight, he was easily irritable and angry over petty issues. In fact, his mental state now affected him physically because he was now vomiting a lot and at times, he was vomiting blood. His health was deteriorating all because he lost the will to live.

Over time, God started strengthening his spirit. He was encouraged to live on and believe he has a purpose, for both him and his children. She told me with a smile on her face at what the power of prayer, counseling, encouragement and God's word can do, she said the last call she made this man told her that he wanted to remarry. She teased him and laughed at how he wants to remarry when he wanted to end his life and they both laughed and celebrated the goodness of God.

He was now a better parent to his kids and his kids' confidence is now stronger and they have a lot of hope and confidence in their dad even though previously it was next to none. They are now more stable and joyful and are doing much better in school. His kids and their future mom also get along well, and it was just a joy to hear of a lovely ending to a sad story like his.

Book 3 - pandemics, disasters and persecutions

18

Pandemics, disasters and persecution

WHY TALK ABOUT IT

Transitioning in a pandemic is yet another confusing way to transition. All the questions that arise in a normal death arise and then some! They are characterized by fear, blame, conspiracy theories and alternative information sources and spiritual interpretation all of which may hardly be true! Dying in a pandemic seems like people have literally been stolen from you almost in an instant.

WHAT THEY ARE

Persecution is hostility and ill treatment that arises due to race, tribal, political or religious beliefs. When we read the pages of history we can see this in the persecution of the early church, in the holocaust, the Rwandan genocide, colonialism around the world and in Africa, the unfair treatment of People of color in America leading to the Black Lives matter Movement and in the persecution of other religious groups in recent times. I can also think of it as general oppression, systemic oppression on various fronts both socially, economically and physically.

Disasters are sudden events causing great damage or loss of life. They range from earthquakes, tsunamis, floods, famines, mudslides and so on.

Pandemics are disastrous events of a medical nature that are widespread and usually cover the world.

WHY DO THEY HAPPEN?

Isn't this the million-dollar question? I bet! But the sad truth is most of the times we don't really know why all these happen isn't it? If we had known the answer to these questions and more so if we had the will and capacity to address them, possibly there might have been no recurrence of them.

Persecution also features in the Bible where the early church was persecuted for their faith in Jesus. It starts with a clash of religious or cultural beliefs between Christianity and Judaism and similarly with other religious or political views in the Roman Empire. We see it culminating in various deaths such as the stoning of Steven in Acts 8, the displacement of the church and later in the gruesome deaths of a majority of the apostles, Christians being sawn in two, being put in boiling oil, and being fed to beastly creatures.

For such pain to be endured there might be some explanation as we know they are suffering for their profession of faith and refusal to denounce their savior. For this we are reminded that we are not only called to believe in Christ but also to suffer for him. No doubt this is confusing, but there is some sense of closure or meaning to it. The disciples and apostles in the book of acts took this as a privilege to suffer for Jesus.

"For you have been given not only the privilege of trusting in Christ but also the privilege of suffering for him." Philippians 1:29 NLT

However, let's not be fooled that this scriptural encouragement lessens the pain because it does not. Many abandon the faith because of the dangers of persecution and so it's impact should not be made light of. However, for those that endure, a crown of life awaits and for them for taking upon themselves the privilege of suffering for Christ.

Disasters include various tragedies also called 'acts of God'. But are they really acts of God? I think the term is generally used for events that man has no control over. However, the term may not be theologically sound. This is because if we go to the beginning of creation God put man on earth to tend and care for it. God gave man the mandate to fill the earth take care and have dominance over it. In a perfect world without sin you would expect this to happen so that we don't destroy our environment in such a manner as to cause global warming and other environmental damage that leads to famines, changing weather patterns and increased environmental catastrophes and in areas with so much smog from pollution, we see an alarming increase in respiratory disorders and illnesses.

In a perfect world, greed and carelessness would not overshadow the need for environmental and societal responsibility and there would be no oil spills by oiling drilling or shipping companies, there would be no explosions of dangerous ammonia nitrate in Beirut for example, nor would other countries with similar stockpiles at the time of the Beirut explosion be at risk such as Senegal, with 2,700 tons, India with 740 tons, Yemen with about 4,900 tons, and even countries like Australia and the United Kingdom who along with other countries are questioning themselves regarding the safety conditions of their ammonia nitrate stockpiles, according to a BBC article dated 21 August 2020.

We see fines levied on companies causing oil spills that destroy nature and the environment and companies such as those in Brazil for causing mudslides that claimed more than 270 lives in 2019 due to failure of their infrastructure. In parts of mineral rich Africa, we would not have the convenient perpetration of rebel wars and civil unrest fueled by foreign forces that swoop in to get all the minerals which they smuggle out of the continent. What are we saying? Some of these challenges are manmade and do not only result from our human failures and errors, but also from greed and wickedness.

A DECAYING WORLD

It may not always be possible to find a specific answer to why each disaster, calamity or pandemic is happening and perhaps I would be foolhardy to attempt that. What we know however is that the original sin of man set the world off balance. Instead of man exercising the delegated rule of God on this earth we see that we ceded our rulership to Satan who became the wicked ruler of this human age and the devil's mission is very clear, 'steal, kill and destroy'.

The cumulative effect of this is a suffering and groaning world. A sick world and a decaying world. One that seeks to be delivered from this spiritual bondage and that cries deep within for freedom.

"the creation looks forward to the day when it will join God's children in glorious freedom from death and decay. For we know that all creation has been groaning as in the pains of childbirth right up to the present time." Romans 8:21-22 NLT

In this decaying world we see a lot of negative consequences, therefore. We see disaster after disaster and catastrophe after catastrophe. Increasingly we see what some would interpret as end times. However, even though we are in the end times, the specific indicators of the very end of the world are yet to manifest. In such an environment therefore, we ought to be well informed and be careful when we try to make sense of things we do not know fully about.

19

Exercising wisdom

AVOIDING PRESUMPTION IN CONFUSING SITUATIONS

Presumption is a dangerous thing for anyone. Presumption leads people to take things for granted. It can also show itself in a sense of arrogance and disrespect to others yourself, disregard to the value of life itself or the honor and repute of others. Mostly, it can lead to disastrous consequences and can make an already bad situation much much worse. In cases of confusion and tragedies God surely does not what us to suffer unnecessarily.

"Enthusiasm without knowledge is no good; haste makes mistakes." Proverbs 19:2 NLT

Sometimes we suffer because we lack knowledge and are simply full of zeal. This can make us do or say things that are unfounded and damaging to say the least. Wisdom, however, is the right application of knowledge and I believe that is what God desires of us. Because when we are wise our actions and words will be wise and wholesome.

We will therefore share some principles that I believe can at least help us to generally avoid presumption.

KNOWING THAT MAN'S KNOWLEDGE IS LIMITED

Man is extremely limited in his knowledge, unlike God who is 'all knowing'. Because of this limitation we can't really explain everything that happens around us or in the world at large. It is presumption to think we can explain everything. Attempting to do so would most likely result in error which can be damaging and destructive to people. That introduces destructive falsehoods which can crush people's lives and faith in God.

It is not uncommon to ascribe disasters to sin or God's judgement. People who say this follow the Puritan approach that believes every catastrophe is as a result of sin. They will point to Sodom and Gomorrah, or similar catastrophes and say let us repent so God may heal our land. However, in a decaying world not everything will be due to sin but simply to the fact that this world has been subjected to futility indeed.

In fact, God's decision in how he deals with sin is different. While Sodom was punished there and then God chooses to reserve judgement for others. An example is the great flood in Genesis 6 where he promised never to destroy the whole world again with water. It's not that sin would not happen again. But because he would now choose to mete judgement on the soul that sins as alternative way of dealing with sin.

"And the Lord was pleased with the aroma of the sacrifice and said to himself, "I will never again curse the ground because of the human race, even though everything they think or imagine is bent toward evil from childhood. I will never again destroy all living things." Genesis 8:21 NLT

Similarly, Jesus bemoaned the sinful cities of Chorazin and Bethsaida and he says though fire and brimstone won't fall on them immediately, their judgement would be worse than that of Sodom and Gomorrah on the judgement day.

"Then Jesus began to denounce the towns where he had done so many of his miracles, because they hadn't repented of their sins and turned to God. "What sorrow awaits you, Korazin and Bethsaida! For if the miracles I did in you had been done in wicked Tyre and Sidon, their people would have repented of their sins long ago, clothing themselves in burlap and throwing ashes on their heads to show their remorse. I tell you, Tyre and Sidon will be better off on judgment day than you." Matthew 11:20-22 NLT

In fact, if truth be told, I believe the people of Sodom and Gomorrah would even marvel at how much more evil the world has become today when we seem to have invented even more sexual freedoms and perversions to the extent of even redefining our sexual orientations. If sin were the only criteria we ought to have been destroyed long ago as soon as these pervasions were invented. And believe you me, they have been around for more than a few decades.

This means that we should not presumptuously ascribe anything happening around us as a result of sin.

It's also not uncommon for people to claim that the world is coming to an end. This remains rhetoric that can lead the world to disrespect the church because of the feeling that the world is not really ending, even though the same message has been preached for many years now. An example is that even in the past half century and even in biblical times the end times message has been preached. While this message remains in principle true, Jesus says that only the father knows the exact dates and times when the end will come. Right know he delays and tarries because he wants as many people to be saved and some of the major things in his calendar are yet to be orchestrated on earth. One of them is the preaching of the gospel of the world and a few other major prophetic events.

MAN'S ABILITY IS LIMITED

Man's limitations mean we can't really control everything that is happening around us. Perhaps some things we can start working towards but it's not always that in the moment we can do something about it because we can't.

Somethings we can stop, and others wen can't for example If your neighborhood is in the path of a tsunami you can't stop the tsunami, if your home is near a forest that has a wild fire that has gone horribly out of control you can't always stop that fire from destroying the neighborhood.

Sometimes if it's your time to die, you can't always stop death, you may prolong life briefly but even after that you might still die. This means sometimes our efforts are limited and though we expend our best efforts, there are limits we cannot cross. We can do all we can to give emergency medical care, we can stabilize someone and hope for the best. Those with chronic illness can be given as much care as possible but due to limits of even modern science, after spending all we can there is only so much that we can do. So, in the Bible, we have the story of the woman with the flow of blood, she spent her life savings but no good came of it because there were limits to what money could do and there were limits to what doctors could do.

COMING TO TERMS

In life we can continually struggle and strive to our own detriment or we can, leave some things to God as the one who understands all things. I think after doing all we can we should leave some things to God. If we don't, I think we can unnecessarily blame ourselves for things we do not need to. Imagine that community destroyed by an earthquake or a mudslide. Imagine someone saying he caused the earthquake maybe because he did not read his Bible or go to church or perhaps, he faltered in other areas of life! What of the doctors who lose patients after trying all they could? After giving assurances that he is now stable and out of the woods? Even medical personnel sometimes wonder at how they have lost some patients.

When we do all we can, we should at times let God be God. We should leave everything else into God's hands.

This does not mean we should not fight gallantly. It simply means after we fight, after we sweat and bleed, we should leave things in God's hands.

This is what David did. He fasted for the life of his son but when he was told his son had died, he left it all in God's hands! In times of pandemic we can sometimes trust God, pray and fast, confess our sins for God to 'heal our land' but still succumb to the pandemic or disaster. At this point let us let God be God. This book's first publication is in a time of a Covid 19 pandemic which has so far claimed 2.2 million lives globally and almost all of the victims I personally know of have someone saying a prayer for them, someone wishing they would get better. Many are fasting for their loved ones; medical doctors are doing all they can to save people's lives, but many are dying in spite of all the gallant efforts.

We can't condemn the sick, we can't demean them and say they don't have the will to live. We can't simply discount and despise the medical staff. We should let God be God in such times.

DON'T BE ANGRY AGAINST GOD

One of the hardest things to do is not to be angry against God. It's so easy to be bitter in times of loss but if we come to the point of letting God be God it means we actually trust him to handle our situations. We can only entrust ourselves and our situations to someone we actually trust. We can't be bitter or angry against God if we are to let him be God!

"Job stood up and tore his robe in grief. Then he shaved his head and fell to the ground to worship. He said, "I came naked from my mother's womb, and I will be naked when I leave. The Lord gave me what I had, and the Lord has taken it away. Praise the name of the Lord!"" Job 1:20-21 NLT

ACKNOWLEDGING THE MYSTERY OF GOD

There are times when we ought to acknowledge the mystery of life and of God. God is mysterious and life is also mysterious at times. That's just how God works.

Part of the mysteriousness of God is his sovereignty:

"Our God is in the heavens, and he does as he wishes."

Psalms 115:3 NLT

Job discovered this when he questioned God. God simply showed him that his ways are higher than man's ways and that God simply knows what he is doing

"Then the Lord answered Job from the whirlwind: "Who is this that questions my wisdom with such ignorant words?" Job 38:1-2 NLT

Moses knew this fact and talked of how we should deal with the mysterious. He said

"The secret things belong unto the Lord our God: but those things which are revealed belong unto us and to our children forever, that we may do all the words of this law." Deuteronomy 29:29 KJV

This is simple but profound wisdom. There are things we should strive for and those we should not. Some secret things should not be striven for or attempted for us to understand.

We should only use what we know or has been made known to us at certain points in time. It does not mean we should not seek to know God's will; it means after seeking God's will and God chooses to hide his will, we should accept that what is secret is not for us to understand.

And in fact, the good news is that we are not answerable for secret and concealed things. The NLT version of the Bible puts this simply and says

""The Lord our God has secrets known to no one. We are not ac-

countable for them, but we and our children are accountable forever for all that he has revealed to us, so that we may obey all the terms of these instructions." Deuteronomy 29:29 NLT

In the justice of God, he will not be so unreasonable as to hold you to account for things that he has chosen to conceal from you.

ACTING RESPONSIBLY

Once we acknowledge the mystery of God we ought to act responsibly. Acting responsibly is about using the available insight and knowledge to do what is right.

The passage we read gives a charge or a command which is for us 'to obey God' with the little he has chosen to reveal to us.

The other charge is not just to 'help ourselves' but also to teach the next generations this important wisdom. So, it's 'for us and our children' to 'obey' him.

What are some of the things we can do in difficult times of tragedy or disaster? We discuss these below.

SEARCHING OUR HEARTS

Firstly, we can set our own lives straight and align them to God. Instead of pointing to the nation and others we ought to introspect and ask God to search us, so that any obvious or hidden sin should be forgiven.

"Search me, O God, and know my heart: try me, and know my thoughts: And see if there be any wicked way in me, and lead me in the way everlasting." Psalms 139:23-24 KJV

Our desire should be to please God and for anything that offends to be pointed out to us. Once we discover any offensive things in us, we should ask for God's mercy and forgiveness.

"Have mercy on me, O God, because of your unfailing love. Because of your great compassion, blot out the stain of my sins. Wash me clean from my guilt. Purify me from my sin." Psalms 51:1-2 NLT

DOING YOUR PART IN THE WORLD

Another way of acting responsibly is simply doing the right things to ensure your safety. In a medical emergency such as a pandemic or any other medical condition there are health guidelines that are given.

In spite of a lot of conspiracy theories, denials and personal opinions it is good to observe the recommended precautionary measures.

When Sodom and Gomorrah were being destroyed Lot was told to leave the city. When the time came, he was actually pulled by the hand to escape the city. In times of trouble sometimes God just wants you to do what is necessary to escape the situation.

Sometimes he simply wants you to be safe and protect yourself in hiding until he tells you otherwise.

For example, he told Moses to build an ark for a torrential rain that would fall over 40 days and cover the earth the responsible thing was for him to build the ark, tell his family and tell his neighborhood about it. Unfortunately, the community around him mocked him and perished. But his responsibility did not just end there. He was also required to save creation by preserving the animals of his day.

God does not want you to save yourself he repeats to us the charge he gave to Adam to tend and keep the garden. The charge remains true to us today as we ought to preserve our environment and ensure that as citizens, leaders and governments we reach out to the disadvantaged, we preserve our environment and protect our planet and together with our governments ensure that we have and adhere to policies, measures and targets that don't destroy our environment. We should therefore fight known issues that cause climate change and global warming and strive for equality, fight poverty and simply do our part.

LOOKING FOR THINGS ABOVE

The Bible says we should look for and set our mind on things that are above. Learning from the mindset of Paul we can share his philosophy that

"For to me, living means living for Christ, and dying is even better." Philippians 1:21 NLT

"For we don't live for ourselves or die for ourselves. If we live, it's to honor the Lord. And if we die, it's to honor the Lord. So, whether we live or die, we belong to the Lord." Romans 14:7-8 NLT

As Christians, we should know that we can be recalled at any time. If disasters, misfortunes, accidents and illnesses have taught us one thing, it's that we can die any time. I recall one of my pastors saying in this time of a pandemic we are experiencing what Job experienced. He had sorry upon sorrow and in fact the enemy did not allow him any breathing space. In about 6 verses of Job 1 from verse 13 to 19 we see about four tragedies happening.

Firstly, all his oxen, donkeys and servants except a sole survivor who told the story were killed, while he was still speaking, another sole survivor told of told of fire from heaven that killed all the sheep and servants, while he was still speaking a survivor talked of camels that were stolen. And as if this was not enough, the confusion of all this simultaneous news, and trying to make sense of the loss of effort, and financial cost, the killer punch was yet to come... and while he was still speaking the fourth survivor told of his 10 children who were smitten and annihilated by a mighty wind that razed their house to the ground in an instant. And just like that all his children were gone in an instant.

But see how the story links the tragedies, while he was told one tragedy, he was hearing of another, and this happened for all four tragedies, 'while he was still speaking' is the prominent phrase in this passage. This is not a mere progression from tragedy to tragedy. This is a string of tragedies. A continuum of such a painful nature as to usher a single fatal blow to the soul of Job! A tsunami of tragedies with such pain and intensity as to crush and pierce his very bones.

That's how life can seem sometimes, I have known of single families losing more than 3 or 4 family members, and some have been orphaned. As they dealt with one tragedy another tragedy occurred and some of these experienced all this within a space of two to six days.

When disaster strikes, we should be like Paul. We should know that we live or die to the Lord. We should be ready to live for God's purposes or die for God's glory. We should know that we can die at any time.

We should not wonder why we have remained, and others have gone, that is God's wish! And this our God, he does whatever he wishes.

20

King above the flood

GOD IS A MIRACULOUS GOD

A king has rule, authority and power over his domain. A king remains king all through the seasons of the year. When we think of pandemics or any of the controversial transitions herein discussed we should remember the fact that God remains King even in these dark seasons of life.

Psalm 29 is an intriguing psalm in my view. It starts with a charge to honor God and ascribe glory to his name.

"Give unto the Lord, O ye mighty, give unto the Lord glory and strength. Give unto the Lord the glory due unto his name; worship the Lord in the beauty of holiness." Psalms 29:1-2 KJV

It then progresses to talk of the mighty deeds of this awesome God, this God who deserves glory and honor and strength.

Six whole verses are dedicated to describing the awe and power of this God.

They talk of how he is a present above all the waters, how he has a thunderous, authoritative and totally majestic voice. Of how, even, mighty cedar trees are split in two like little twigs or match sticks. How his voice makes the enemy to skip away from his presence, how he shakes our wilderness and intervenes in dry situations, and how he brings productivity in our lives.

And it culminates in verse 9 whereby all who are in his glorious temple fall down in worship and adoration as they proclaim 'glory, glory, strength and power are yours'. What a mighty God. This is the God we serve he is a mighty God!

THE PARADOXICAL GOD

There is however verse ten of this chapter. It talks of this God as God of the flood.

Uh oh! Floods are not nice. They bring destruction of life and property. Noah's flood annihilated the earth and, in our day, and time many other flood waters destroy homes and livelihoods. Floods are not nice. They can be gradual, but others are flash floods which are sudden and unannounced. They can destroy your harvest, all your financial and social investments. They can bring immense pain.

But this God announces himself as being enthroned as king over the flood! And, herein is the paradox and the mystery and, to many of us going through the floods of life, here is the anti-climax. We don't like the flood at all and yet to this God we owe the charge to

'Honor him

'Lift him up

'Worship him and declare his glory!

Will you whine and complain with me, as most humans do, when called to worship this God in the flood? Or am I the only one who struggles to worship in difficult times? It's ok to feel lost, to feel anger and pain and depression. It's ok if you have felt despair! Look at Job, he was in so much pain that he rent his robe in the pain that was bubbling from his gut. But, gritting his teeth, he worships God! He squeezes out an ounce of reverence which turns into full blown worship to his God and King.

"Then Job arose, and rent his mantle, and shaved his head, and fell down upon the ground, and worshipped," Job 1:20 KJV

"Give unto the Lord, O ye mighty, give unto the Lord glory and strength." Psalms 29:1 KJV

How is God King over the flood?

This question is not a simple one to answer but we can start with talking about power and his might, but that has already been touted. But, how is he king when things go wrong? These are discussed in the following paragraphs.

GOD IS NOT UNAWARE

Amidst the confusion of loss in any tragedy is the comfort that God is all knowing! Can you imagine God talking to your loved one in heaven

'Bill are you also here?

When did you get here?

How did you get here?

But how come I was not told of this?

Which angel was responsible for bringing you here?

Is that a god you can have confidence in? Not at all? Such a god would be a fraud not worth our worship and reverence. Such a god would be sleeping on the job! But our God doesn't sleep on the job!

"Behold, He who keeps Israel Will neither slumber [briefly] nor sleep [soundly]." Psalms 121:4 AMP

So how do bad things happen? I think the answer is in Mathew 10:29.

"Are not two little sparrows sold for a copper coin? And yet not one of them falls to the ground apart from your Father's will." Matthew 10:29 AMP

I can't claim to know why bad things happen to good people.

Sometimes we will find various reasons, perhaps that it's God's will, perhaps that it's to preserve us from future danger and even that all things work together for God. This I cannot dispute because there are scriptures that talk of these things. Whether properly or misapplied that is a matter for another day.

But you will agree with me that some tragedies are so confusing, traumatic, gruesome, senseless and sometimes too diabolical to comprehend completely.

When this happens, all I can tell you is that your God was not sleeping when this happened! I think we can agree on that, and that your God is not dead! Not at all

I would also like to say that if God can see and permit the sparrow to fall and die, he is definitely involved in the fall of his human creation and more so his children who trust in him, and even more his servants who serve him in whatever capacity.

This is very important to note because in times of calamity both good and bad people fall in death. The world takes this as an opportunity to mock believers and say, you should have known better! You should have been more cautious.

Instead of answering them let's be quiet and know that he is God even in the storm, let's also know that God was not clueless, oblivious and unaware of their death, but, in fact, that he even allowed it to happen. Remember, your God never slumbers! And as far as allowing things to happen, we see this when he allowed the devil to assault Job and when he gave him clear limits of what should happen. Friends,

'God is in control!'

GOD DOES NOT NEED TO WIN ALL HIS BATTLES

Unlike you and I, who would like to make it a point that we win every battle we wage, God is not like that. He sees no need to win each battle because he has already won the war. In fact, the mystery of his victory is in his apparent defeat.

God was king of the flood and did not see the need to let Jesus win the legal accusations laid on him by the Sanhedrin. Jesus saw no need to avoid being mocked, scourged and whipped with a scorpion whip that tore through his flesh.

God was king of the flood when Jesus was crucified in a napkin. Actually, we like to think of the napkin because this is supposedly done to ensure a bit of modesty to him, but in reality, it is believed that in true Roman tradition, he would have been crucified literally naked. But God was still king of the flood then!

Can you imagine living in the same time and space as Jesus the messiah? What mighty miracles would you experience? And imagine John the Baptist who was killed while Jesus was alive and well! This the same John who was commended by Jesus as the greatest prophet of all time and the greatest of any born of a woman and yet this prophet was unjustly slain and beheaded.

I submit to you that God was king of the flood when John was decapitated, and his bloody head rolled on the ground.

This is so important because we think of God's servants as having special protection and privilege. And indeed, in times of pandemics many servants of God lose their lives. Already, I know of about a dozen or so true servants of God who have lost their lives in the current pandemic. All very prominent and even our own church pastor. But even in such times God remains king over the flood!

God was king of the flood when Jesus stood before Pilate under threat that he could do whatever he wishes to Jesus. The king of the flood simply highlighted that even this authority he is bragging about was given to him by the King of the flood!

"So, Pilate said to Him, "You do not speak to me? Do You not know that I have authority to release You, and I have authority to crucify You?" Jesus answered, "You would have no authority over Me at all if it had not been given to you from above. For this reason the sin and guilt of the one who handed Me over to you is greater [than your own]."" John 19:10-11 AMP

So, don't despair when you are abused. Just know that your abusers will answer to God on how they have used the power given to them by the king of the flood.

He does not despair when his own are slain

In our humanity we despair in loss! But not God. God's objectives are not our objectives.

""Now My soul is troubled and deeply distressed; what shall I say?

'Father, save Me from this hour [of trial and agony]'? But it is for this [very] purpose that I have come to this hour [this time and place]." John 12:27 AMP

"So, Pilate said to Him, "Then You are a King?" Jesus answered, "You say [correctly] that I am a King. This is why I was born, and for this I have come into the world, to testify to the truth. Everyone who is of the truth [who is a friend of the truth and belongs to the truth] hears and listens carefully to My voice."" John 18:37 AMP

When Christians fall God does not jump out of his skin because he has a home prepared for them. A glorious home! He has a reward waiting for them one he so desperately wishes to give to his children. God did not despair when John was beheaded, or when the prophets of old were killed. He knew the death of Jesus was the key to victory. When the apostles were beheaded and put in boiling oil or crucified upside down, he did not despair and send legions of angels to save Jesus and make a point! He knew their course was done and their race was ran! He did not need to 'save face'. Remember

'To live is Christ and to die is gain'

"If we live, we live for the Lord, and if we die, we die for the Lord. So then, whether we live or die, we are the Lord's. For Christ died and lived again for this reason, that He might be Lord of both the dead and the living." Romans 14:8-9 AMP

In God's eyes living and dying are the same to him. It's all for his purposes and secondly, Jesus is Lord both here on earth and in heaven! He is Lord of the living on earth and of the dead who actually are alive in heaven.

The king of the flood is king everywhere, his domain is not

limited to heaven but also on earth. If he was only God on this earth, he truly would not be God at all.

"This is what the LORD says, "Heaven is My throne and the earth is My footstool" Isaiah 66:1 AMP

God simply fills all in all, he exists in heaven and on earth. He literally fills all in all.

In fact, the death of the righteousness in his eyes is precious

"Precious [and of great consequence] in the sight of the LORD Is the death of His godly ones [so He watches over them]." Psalms 116:15 AMP

In fact, the death of the righteous is so precious that Balaam the false prophet hired to curse Israel, actually prayed to die the death of the righteous.

"Who can count the dust (the descendants) of Jacob and the number of even the fourth part of Israel? Let me die the death of the righteous [those who are upright and in right standing with God], And let my end be like his!"" Numbers 23:10 AMP

While we despair of how our loved ones have gone to be with the Lord, the Bible says their death is precious in God's eyes. This is because he never loses his children and you can therefore be encouraged that God is indeed in control and enthroned as king over the flood!

21

The king will strengthen you

HE GIVES STRENGTH TO HIS PEOPLE

One great promise we have is that no matter how devastated we are, God promises to strengthen you!

Strength comes from the fact that he perfects his strength in our weakness. It also comes from the fact that he is with us! And he never forsakes us.

He is our shepherd and indeed God will guide and strengthen us.

"The LORD is my light and my salvation; Whom shall I fear? The

LORD is the strength of my life; Of whom shall I be afraid?" Psalms 27:1 NKJV

"The LORD will give strength to His people; The LORD will bless His people with peace." Psalms 29:11 NKJV

The promise we have from God is that he will strengthen us with his presence and his word. The fact that God alone is with you means you have strength. The fact that Emmanuel is in your heart means you will not falter.

GOD WILL GIVE YOU PEACE

Another great promise is that we will also have peace. Now this is not easy in time of tragedy. But God says his people will be surrounded with peace. Peace comes from simply knowing that

'God is with you
God is your defense
God is king over the flood
We are not lost
We remain in God's hands
We can cast our cares on him
We have a home and heaven is that home!

Once we know this, God's peace infuses and flows into our hearts like a stream. The prince of peace Jesus will encourage and take away fear from our hearts. He will take away despair and give us hopeful expectation

May God strengthen you in your loss
May he strengthen you in your tragedy
May he be a refuge and fortress in your storm
May you know him as king of the flood

May you know him and see him as enthroned over the flood with majesty, with power and authority.

"and the peace of God, which surpasses all understanding, will guard your hearts and minds through Christ Jesus." Philippians 4:7 NKJV

Ascribe glory and strength to the king of the flood

Finally, we ought to obey the call and charge to worship God and ascribe glory honor and strength to God.

"Give unto the LORD, O you mighty ones, Give unto the LORD glory and strength. Give unto the LORD the glory due to His name; Worship the LORD in the beauty of holiness." Psalms 29:1-2 NKJV

I think we should obey and worship him when he does the miraculous and spectacular and also worship him when he brings us through the flood.

We should be like Job who worships even when we are slain.

"Though he slay me, yet will I trust in him: but I will maintain mine own ways before him." Job 13:15 KJV

Like Habakkuk, we should pledge to praise God in whatever situation

"Although the fig tree shall not blossom, neither shall fruit be in the vines; the labour of the olive shall fail, and the fields shall yield no meat; the flock shall be cut off from the fold, and there shall be no herd in the stalls: Yet I will rejoice in the Lord, I will joy in the God of my salvation." Habakkuk 3:17-18 KJV

Join me in this pledge,

I will rejoice in God my savior

I will encourage myself in the Lord

In spite of my loss

In spite of my tragedy

In spite of my disappointment.

I will rejoice because my salvation is not only in God but even if it does. It come and I die in faith, my salvation and reward is God himself and perhaps nothing else.

This oh Lord is my pledge.

22

A prayer for strength

Dear Father God,

I come to you because I feel overwhelmed, for the floodwaters have come up to my neck. I feel like I'm sinking deeper and deeper into a muddy swamp. My feet are slippery, and I can't find my grip. I am in deep waters and the flood overwhelms me!

I feel drained from crying and my throat is dry, my eyes are sore and swollen from weeping, but I wait for you to help me. So, I keep praying to you, Lord, hoping and trusting that you will show me favor and unfailing love.

Answer my prayer with your sure salvation. Rescue me from the mud, don't let me sink any deeper, rescue me from the enemy. Answer my prayers, O Lord, for your unfailing love is wonderful, your hand is strong and mighty, it holds me and lifts me up, up from the deep waters, up from the muddy clay, up from the pit of death. And this thing I know, I will see your goodness, oh God, in this land of the living. I will not die but live and declare your wonders oh Lord!

In Jesus name I have prayed... Amen

23

A prayer for others

Dear Father God,

I come to you on behalf of my children and family and all who are at risk of succumbing to suicidal thoughts. I sprinkle the blood of Jesus on them. The blood that speaks better things than the blood of Abel. On their and my own behalf I confess all the sins of our forefathers, both known and unknown! Forgive and have mercy on us oh Lord!

I also pray for those who are tormented by suicidal thoughts and actual suicides in their family. Lord, I bring them to your cross. May they know you as Lord and Savior. May the power of the cross destroy the curse of suicide in their bloodline. May every curse be destroyed because Jesus has already become a curse on our behalf, theirs and mine!

Have mercy on those that are hopeless. let the blood of Jesus speak for them, let it speak mercy, forgiveness and grace! Let vengeance be done away with, let no blood be spilt, let no life be lost! Let the anointing of the Holy Spirit break the yoke of suicide and let them hope in you oh Lord. Let them know they will see your goodness in the land of the living! Satan has no hold on me and them, and I shall live and declare your mighty works!

In Jesus name I have prayed... Amen

24

A prayer for salvation

Dear Jesus,
You have said that "I am the way, the truth and the life".
Today I choose to believe that indeed you are the way to heaven, the way to my heavenly father, you are the truth of the world and you are my life!
I believe you have gone to heaven to prepare a place for me
To prepare room for me in your father's house
You have said "there are many rooms in my father's house" and "where I am going you will be also."
Jesus, I want to go to heaven I want to come home after this life. I want to come to my father in heaven!
Therefore, I ask for the forgiveness of my sins through
The shed blood of Jesus as the only atonement for my sin
I confess with my mouth that Jesus you are the Lord of my life and I receive you as my personal savior

I believe that you rose again from the dead
I thank you that you have forgiven my sin and written my name in the book of life
In Jesus name I have prayed... Amen!

Name ....
Date ....

www.ingramcontent.com/pod-product-compliance
Ingram Content Group UK Ltd.
Pitfield, Milton Keynes, MK11 3LW, UK
UKHW040021200726
13854UKWH00001B/298

9 789990 809282